# SKILLS IN
# TEXTILES
# TECHNOLOGY

## Rose Sinclair

Heinemann Educational Publishers
Halley Court, Jordan Hill, Oxford OX2 8EJ
a division of Reed Educational & Professional
Publishing Ltd

OXFORD FLORENCE PRAGUE MADRID
ATHENS MELBOURNE AUCKLAND
KUALA LUMPUR SINGAPORE TOKYO
IBADAN NAIROBI KAMPALA
JOHANNESBURG GABORONE
PORTSMOUTH NH (USA) CHICAGO
MEXICO CITY SAO PAULO

Text © Rose Sinclair, 1997

First published 1997

01 00 99 98 97

10 9 8 7 6 5 4 3 2 1

British Library Cataloguing in Publication Data

A catalogue record for this book is available from
the British Library

ISBN 0 435 42114 X

Designed and typeset by Dennis Fairey
& Associates Ltd

Illustrated by Arthur Phillips, Piers Sanford and
Bill Lisle

Printed and bound in Spain by Mateu Cromo

## Acknowledgements

The publishers would like to thank the following for
permission to reproduce copyright material:

Blackwell Scientific Publications for the information
and illustration on **page 62** and the table on
**page 63**; Burton Group for the label information
on **page 52**; Coats Viyella Stevensons for the
information on **page 22**; Courtaulds Plc for the
information on **page 16**; Marks & Spencer for the
label information on **page 52**; Next Plc for the label
information on **page 52**; McGraw-Hill for the case
study on **page 67**; Shima Seiki Europe for the
information and illustration on **page 79**; Thames &
Hudson for the extract from the poem, *Colour
Harmony 2* by Bride Whelan, on **page 18**.

The publishers wish to thank the following for
permission to use photographs:

**page 5**: Zefa (top), Warren Williams/Zefa (centre),
Duncan Maxwell/Robert Harding Picture Library
(bottom); **page 8**: Science Photo Library (bottom,
top left), Andrew Syred/Science Photo Library
(bottom, top right), Sidney Moulds/Science Photo
Library (bottom, bottom left), Manfred Kage (bottom,
bottom right); **page 9**: House of Hemp (bottom),
Dupont (top left), Gore-Tex (top centre), Tencel
(top right); **page 12**: Eddie Mulholland/ Gamma/
Frank Spooner Pictures; **page 14**: Ruddingtons
Framework and Knitters Museum (left), Mary Evans
Picture Library (right); **page 15**: E T Archive (left),
Mary Evans Picture Library (right); **page 16**:
Courtaulds Textiles; **page 20**: Skopos Designs Ltd
(top), Linda Nottingham (centre), Annie Black
(bottom); **page 21**: Dylon (top, top left), Linda
Nottingham (top, bottom right), Patrick Gorman,
Embroiders Guild (bottom), Janome (right); **page
23**: Chris Honeywell (top), NEC Arnold ( bottom);
**page 24**: Janome; **page 28**: Robert Harding Picture
Library; **page 32**: Annie Black (top), Linda
Nottingham (centre); **page 33**: Chris Honeywell;
**page 34**: Shima Seiki Europe; **page 36**: Chris
Honeywell; **page 41**: Chris Honeywell; **page 44**:
Trevor Hill (top), Chris Honeywell (3 photos);
**page 47**: Philippe Poulet/Robert Harding Picture
Library (top left), Sally and Richard Greenhill (top
centre), IPC Magazines/Robert Harding Picture
Library (top right), Peugeot (bottom left), Gray
Mortimore/Allsport (bottom right); **page 51**: Gore-
Tex; **page 53**: Gore-Tex, SympaTex; **page 59**:
Trevor Hill (A), Liaison International/Robert
Harding Picture Library (B), Trevor Clifford (C),
J Allan Cash (D), Trevor Hill (E), IPC Magazines/
Robert Harding Picture Library (F), Sally and
Richard Greenhill (G), House of Hemp (H); **page 60**:
IPC Magazines/Robert Harding Picture Library
(left), Kodak/Robert Harding Picture Library (right);
**page 61**: Chris Honeywell (top), Clark's Shoes
(bottom); **page 65**: Chris Honeywell; **page 66**:
Selfridges; **page 67**: Burton Group; **page 72**:
Katherine Hamnett (left), Tencel (right); **page 73**:
E T Archive (left), Pauline Burbridge, Embroiders
Guild (right); **page 74**: Niall McInernary (left), Sally
and Richard Greenhill (right); **page 75**: Lizzey Reakes;
**page 77**: Microspot (right); **page 78**: Lectra Systems;
**page 79**: Shima Seiki Europe; **page 80**: Vivienne
Westwood; **page 84**: E T Archive (left), Philip
O'Reilly (right); **page 85**: Linda Nottingham; **page
88**: Chris Honeywell; **page 89**: Louis Vuitton (top
left), Chris Honeywell (bottom left), Mary Evans
Picture Library (right); **page 93** Niall McInernary
(left and top right); Chris Honeywell (bottom right).

The publishers thank Aricot Vert Designs for
permission to reproduce the cover photograph.

The publishers have made every effort to trace
copyright holders.

# Contents

# What is textiles technology?

## What are textiles?

Textiles play an important part in our lives, and are essential to our well being and comfort. They can be used for protection, eg clothing, or for decoration, eg wall-hangings, and are used by different cultures all over the world in different ways. So what are textiles? The term was originally used to describe **woven** or **knitted fabrics.** However, nowadays the word textiles is often used to describe any product made from fabric, whether woven, knitted or **bonded.**

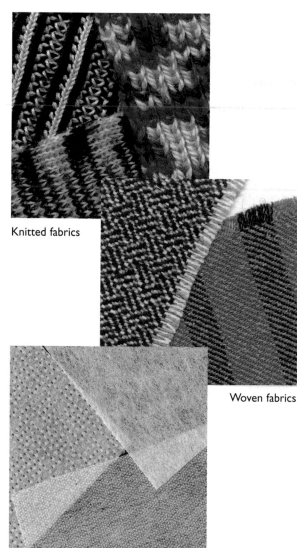

Knitted fabrics

Woven fabrics

Bonded fabrics (non-woven)

## To do

**1** Look at each room in your home. How many items can you name that are made from textiles? Note how many are made from woven, knitted or bonded fabrics. What do your results show? How do they compare with others in your class? Display your findings using a bar chart. You could use a computer spreadsheet program or database to do this.

**2** Investigate other materials that are found in your home. Compare them with the results of your textiles investigation. Display your findings using a pie chart. What do your results show? Did your findings surprise you? Now you will probably start to see how important textiles are!

**3** Now look at the clothing you are wearing. How many items do you have that are made out of either woven, knitted or bonded fabrics? Display your findings. Store all the information you have gathered on a computer database for later use.

## What is textiles technology all about?

Textiles technology is all about using your knowledge and skills to plan, design and make good quality textiles products.

Here are some of the topics you will cover when studying textiles technology:

- analysing design briefs
- creating specifications for a given textiles product
- testing textiles products
- disassembling textiles products
- physical and chemical properties of textiles
- costing a textiles product

- using information technology in designing and making a textiles product
- investigating the labelling and packaging on textiles products
- quality control and quality assurance
- industrial textiles production on a large scale
- exploring craft techniques and their relationship to modern technology.

There are lots of activities in this book. These can be used:

- as Design and Make Activities (DMAs)
- as Focused Practical Tasks (FPTs) and activities which will enable you to investigate, disassemble and evaluate ideas which are all part of the National Curriculum, Design and Technology.

Textiles technology can help you to understand how textiles products are made and the processes involved. It will enable you to understand the different **visual** (look of) and **tactile** (feel of) **properties of fibres and fabrics**, as well as other properties, such as warmth and absorbency, and how you can use these features when you plan, design and make your own textiles products.

Textiles technology is also about how to make textiles products that can perform in all sorts of conditions and in all sorts of circumstances. For example, woven or knitted fabric can be manufactured to make it stronger or give it improved qualities or to help it to stand up to lots of wear and tear. Manufacturers can also use different methods of production, such as mixing and blending fibres, as a way of making an expensive fabric cheaper.

Advances in textiles technology have meant that textiles can be used in many different ways. For example:

- in road construction – these are called **geotextiles**
- for medical purposes such as bandages and wound dressings that dissolve when in contact with the skin – this is called **biotechnology** or **biotextiles.**

A fireman in protective clothing

A diver in a wet suit

A climber dressed for cold conditions

Some textiles designed for special uses

## Questions

**1** What is textiles technology? Explain it in your own words.

**2** Make a list of other uses of textiles outside the home. In what ways, if any, do these differ? What other properties do these textiles products need in order to be used? For example, fabrics used for tents need to be strong, waterproof and able to withstand very hot or very cold temperatures. To meet these requirements tent fabrics should be woven and treated to make them waterproof.

# Knowledge and skills

## What do you need to know?

The chart shows some of the practical skills and knowledge you will need when planning and making a quality textiles product.

| Skills | Examples |
| --- | --- |
| Planning | Making detailed plans of work needed to make a complete product, including drawings of particular aspects of your product, eg making a pocket |
| Measuring accurately | Using correct measuring tools such as rulers and tape measures |
| Using tools and equipment accurately and safely | Learning how to use a range of different sewing machines, eg overlocker, computerised sewing machines |
| Testing products | Testing fabrics and evaluating results and making changes if necessary |
| Assembling products accurately | Joining together the parts of an item that you have made in the correct order to achieve a quality finish |

**Designing skills**

- Make plan of work
- Use computer software to design products
- Evaluate products
- Use information technology to create ideas
- Test products to check quality of work at crucial points
- Consider design attributes:
  - aesthetic, visual qualities – appearance
  - aesthetic, tactile qualities – drape, texture
- Design products for manufacture of single item and in large quantities
- Develop specifications

**Making skills**

- Understand the difference between quality control and quality assurance and how they are used in the making process
- Evaluate products
- Modify (change) product to meet end use
- Add finishing techniques
- Produce step-by-step plan for making product. Include detailed instructions for difficult areas using pictures and words
- Use a range of processes to join fabrics together
- Use correct tools and equipment for the job

The two diagrams (above) and the one opposite (top left) show some of the skills and knowledge needed for making and designing textiles products

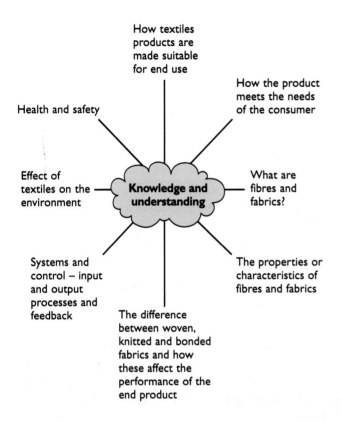

How textiles products are made suitable for end use

How the product meets the needs of the consumer

Health and safety

Effect of textiles on the environment

**Knowledge and understanding**

What are fibres and fabrics?

Systems and control – input and output processes and feedback

The properties or characteristics of fibres and fabrics

The difference between woven, knitted and bonded fabrics and how these affect the performance of the end product

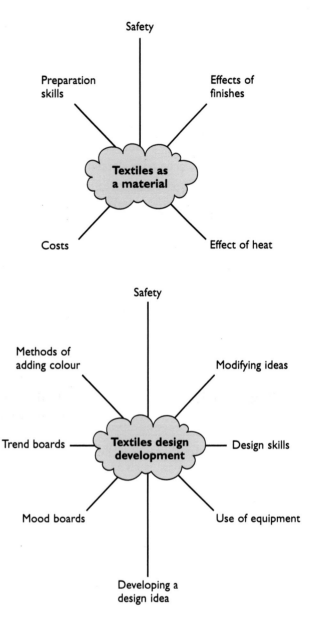

Safety

Preparation skills

Effects of finishes

**Textiles as a material**

Costs

Effect of heat

Safety

Methods of adding colour

Modifying ideas

Trend boards

**Textiles design development**

Design skills

Mood boards

Use of equipment

Developing a design idea

## Textiles product development

Manufacturers use different skills when developing textiles products. You will need some of these, too. This book looks at some of them. The spider diagrams include the pages where you will find these topics dealt with more fully.

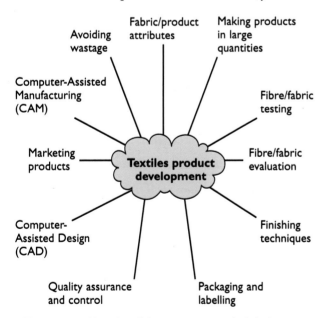

Avoiding wastage

Fabric/product attributes

Making products in large quantities

Computer-Assisted Manufacturing (CAM)

Fibre/fabric testing

Marketing products

**Textiles product development**

Fibre/fabric evaluation

Computer-Assisted Design (CAD)

Finishing techniques

Quality assurance and control

Packaging and labelling

The diagram (above) and the two opposite (right) show skills linked to textiles product development

# Fibres and fabrics

Textiles technology is about using **yarns** and making them into fabrics, adding colours and then turning the fabrics into finished products. But you will also need to understand how yarns are made, and the processes involved in making **fibres** into yarns and then into fabrics.

## Fibres

Fibres are the raw materials of textiles. They are hair-like structures that are spun into yarns. Fibres are divided into three main types:

- **Natural fibres** come from sources such as plants and animals, eg cotton, wool.
- **Synthetic fibres** are made from chemicals such as oil, eg nylon, polyester, acrylic.
- **Man-made** or **regenerated fibres** are made from a combination of natural and synthetic resources, such as wood and chemicals, eg viscose, rayon, tencel.

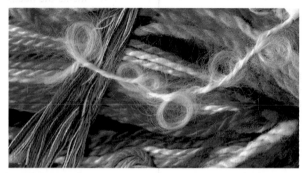

Different types of yarn

Fibres under the microscope: dacron polyester (top left), silk (top right), nylon (bottom left) and lambswool (bottom right).

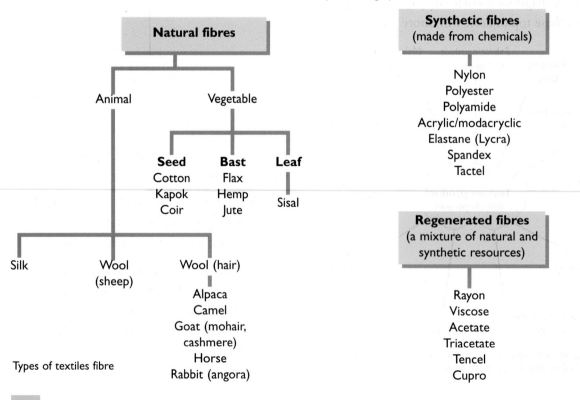

Types of textiles fibre

**Natural fibres**

Animal — Vegetable

**Seed**
Cotton
Kapok
Coir

**Bast**
Flax
Hemp
Jute

**Leaf**
Sisal

Silk — Wool (sheep) — Wool (hair)
Alpaca
Camel
Goat (mohair, cashmere)
Horse
Rabbit (angora)

**Synthetic fibres**
(made from chemicals)

Nylon
Polyester
Polyamide
Acrylic/modacryclic
Elastane (Lycra)
Spandex
Tactel

**Regenerated fibres**
(a mixture of natural and synthetic resources)

Rayon
Viscose
Acetate
Triacetate
Tencel
Cupro

Each type of fibre has its own **properties** or characteristics which makes it suitable for particular jobs. By looking at fibre properties and how fibres react in certain conditions, technologists can see how to alter the properties and create a new improved fabric. For example, fibres can be **blended** or **mixed** together. An example of a blended fibre is cotton polyester which is used for lightweight clothing such as shirts. It is usually blended in a 45/65% combination, so that the best fabric quality and the ideal properties are used to make the product.

## Creating new fabrics

Technologists also look at alternative sources of fibre such as using pineapple leaves or banana leaves and at different ways of cultivating plants and then using the fibres to create fabrics that look good and are environmentally friendly.

One such fibre is hemp, used in textiles since the sixteenth century, primarily for clothing and bedding. Cotton fabric became more popular for clothing, hemp was used less. Today this strong fibre is usually made into rope and sacking. Its hardwearing qualities are well known – the first Levi jeans that were produced were made from hemp fabric.

Hemp is now being developed by technologists as a fibre of the future for clothing. Hemp can be grown organically, without using fungicides, pesticides or herbicides. It only needs small amounts of fertiliser and water, and can be grown in most parts of the world. Hemp can be mixed

with other fibres such as silk and cotton, and is available in different weights so it can be used for jackets, canvas bags and shoes and lightweight shirts, skirts and blouses.

Hemp is an eco-friendly fibre

## The new generation of fibres and fabrics

Technologists may combine several fibres together in a single fabric, or combine several layers of fabric. Current technology is so advanced that technologists have created yarns called **microfibres** that are thinner than a single strand of hair. These can be used to make lightweight fabrics that have a variety of end uses, such as Lycra, Gore-Tex and Tencel.

Lycra

Tencel

Gore-Tex

### To do

**1** Make a list of the textiles products that you wear and ones that are found around the home. How many are made up of two or more different fibres? Display your findings, listing the combinations. Do you think that this makes a difference to the way that the garments or other textiles products feel? Give three reasons for your answer. Do you think they perform better in combinations? Give three reasons for your answer.

**2** Using magazines and other sources of information, such as catalogues, find pictures of textiles products that use various fibre combinations. Create an information board to display what you have found out. What is the most popular fibre combination? Which textiles products is this combination found in? Give reasons for your answers.

# How fabrics are made

The process of changing fibres into yarns is called **conversion.** Let's look at how the fabric for a cotton shirt is made.

1 The raw fibre – the ripe cotton balls – are harvested and sorted. The seeds are removed and the cotton boll is broken down.

2 The raw cotton fibre is broken down in a machine called a **gin.**

3 The cotton fibres are taken to a spinning mill where they are twisted into yarn by a process called **spinning.** Yarn is twisted into either an 'S' or a 'Z' twist depending on its end use. The yarn is continually checked for faults and to make sure it has the right twist. Colour may be added during fibre processing or after the yarn is spun.

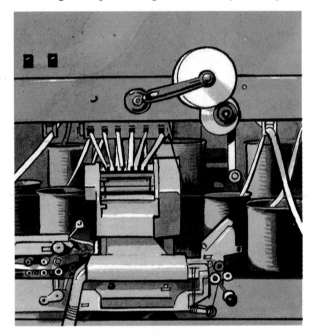

**4** The finished yarn is taken to a fabric manufacturer to be made into fabric. Fabric may be woven or knitted. (There are also **non-woven** or **bonded** fabrics.) The process used to change the yarn into fabric for the shirt is called **weaving.** Weaving is done on a machine called a **loom.** An electronic high-speed loom is used to weave the fabric of the shirt. Several sample lengths of fabric are produced and tested to make sure they are of the correct quality.

**5** After weaving, the fabric is checked to ensure there are no faults such as knots or loose threads. If a fabric has too many faults, it is rejected and may be sold as seconds. Fabrics at this stage are called **greige** or **grey goods.**

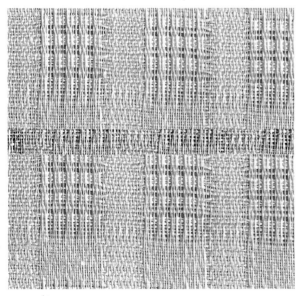

An example of woven fabric

**6** The fabric still has a lot of impurities and oil in it. It now enters the **production stage** where it is cleaned in a process called **scouring.** Colour may be added to the fabric by **dyeing** or **printing** at this stage. The fabric can then go through the final cleaning process. This is called **finishing.** It is now ready to be made into a product.

**To do**

Using the information on these pages, make a simple flow chart showing the six stages in the processing of a fibre into a fabric. To do this you will need to write down each stage in a box. The first stage has been done for you below.

> The raw fibre is harvested

⬇

11

# Making fabrics into textiles products

Most of the textiles products we use are made on a large scale in manufacturing plants. These products are called **wholesale goods** or **mass-produced goods.** They are found in most high street shops, such as Marks & Spencer and BHS, and are generally inexpensive to buy. Textiles products made on a small scale by crafts people are sold at much higher prices because they cost a lot more to make than mass-produced goods. This is because much fewer items are made and the cost of labour and materials is higher.

**Haute couture** companies make single one-off garments. Their clothes are made of the highest quality fabrics, which have to be specially ordered and cost thousands of pounds. Famous haute couture designers include Christian Dior, Alexander McQueen, Ralph Lauren and Vivienne Westwood.

The designer Alexander McQueen fitting a dress

## The textiles product design chain

All textiles products go through a number of stages. This is called the textiles product design chain. Here is one for a cotton shirt.

Design concept is proposed
⬇
Market research is carried out to identify the market for the shirt and what features it should have
⬇
Design brief is produced and design ideas are drawn up
⬇
Sample design is made
⬇
Initial costings are made
⬇
Pattern is modified
⬇
Specification to ensure that shirt produced is of correct quality and testing procedures for each stage of production are drawn up
⬇
Production schedule is set
⬇
Shirt is manufactured and packaged
⬇
Shirt is delivered to customer

## Manufacturing a cotton shirt

The **manufacturing stage** involves making the fabric into the final product. Let's look at how a cotton shirt is made.

1 After market research has been done, a design brief for the shirt is drawn up and given to the designer. Using this and other information, the designer produces a range of ideas.

2 Two or three design ideas are made into sample shirts using calico. This is called a **toile.** The design is altered if necessary. The pattern is graded into the sizes needed, and the number of stages involved in making the shirt and how much it will cost to make are worked out. The shirt is then made by a sample machinist in the chosen fabric.

**3** Once the design is approved, it can be sent to the manufacturer with making-up instructions. The pattern pieces are laid on the fabric in such a way as to avoid wastage. This can be worked out using a specialist computer program, and the fabric is cut out.

**4** The production schedule is worked out, and then each part of the shirt is sent in pieces to different workstations to be sewn in different parts. A random sample is taken from each workstation to ensure that the sewn pieces are made up correctly and are of the correct quality.

**5** Once the complete shirt is made, a final inspection is carried out before pressing.

**6** The shirt is packaged and sent to the retailer for selling to the consumer.

## To do

**1** Gather together information about different types of textiles products. This may be in the form of fabric samples or pictures. Put the information you have gathered into a table like the one below.

| Type of fabric (woven/knitted/printed) | Possible fibre content | What is the fabric used for? | Other possible end uses | Design features of the fabric (colours, patterns etc.) |
|---|---|---|---|---|
|  |  |  |  |  |

**2** What similarities did you notice in the types of fabric that you found? (For example, some fabrics may be used only for clothing and others for furnishing). Why do you think this is?

**3** Using magazines, eg *Vogue*, newspapers and history of costume books, investigate the work of a famous haute couture designer. Present your work in the form of a report. Include illustrations.

# How the textiles industry developed

The chart shows how textiles became part of everyday life and how new technology has influenced the changes that have taken place in the production of fibres, yarns and fabrics.

| The development of the textiles industry | |
|---|---|
| Before 5000 BC | Prehistoric people use animal skins to make clothing |
| 5000–3000 BC | Skills in spinning, weaving and dyeing first developed. People start to embroider and decorate fabrics |
| 3000 BC | Linen woven in Egypt. Cotton spun in India. In the cold climate of northern Europe wool fabric in common use |
| 3rd century AD | Textiles industry in Britain. The Romans build first weaving mill in south-west England |
| 12th century | Silk woven and spun in China. Over the next few centuries the textiles industry remains a cottage industry |
| 14th–17th centuries | The textiles industry grows. Women mainly do the spinning, men are in charge of weaving |
| 1589 | **Knitting machine** invented by William Lee |
| Early 18th century | Cotton industry beginning to grow in Lancashire |
| 1733 | **Flying shuttle** invented by John Kay. By 1760 the shuttle is in general use in the cotton industry |
| 1764–79 | Spinning speeded up by invention of the **spinning jenny** by James Hargreaves in 1764, the **water frame** by Richard Arkwright in 1769 and the **spinning mule** by Samuel Crompton in 1779 |
| 19th century | Textiles industry continues to grow. Further progress in the printing of fabrics. **Sewing machine** invented. The start of mass-produced clothing and other textiles products. The famous artist and textile designer **William Morris** (1834–96) founds a company to make furniture, tapestries, carpets and furnishing materials. |
| 1907 | The artificial silk fibre Rayon is produced and used for clothing and underwear |

An early knitting machine

A flying shuttle

One of the first sewing machines

| 1925 | Acetate is used for dresses and jacket linings |
|---|---|
| 1939 | Nylon produced. Used for stockings and parachute material |
| 1950 | Elastane fibre, used in ladies' underwear and elastic, introduced. Today called Lycra |
| 1956 | Acrylic and polyester introduced to Britain. Used mainly for clothing |
| 1970s | Bonded fibres used in carpet and blanket manufacture |
| 1956–96 | Over 40 new fibres developed |
| 1990s | Computer technology revolutionises design and manufacture of textiles. New hi-tech fibres created and developed as a response to consumer/end user needs |

A William Morris tapestry

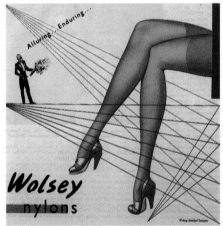

Early use of nylon for stockings

## To do

**1** From the information given in the chart, make a time-line highlighting the main areas of development in the textiles industry.

**2** Which were the main fibres used in textiles up to the beginning of the twentieth century? Give three reasons for your answer.

**3** Find some pictures of textiles products of the past and present which are made from these fibres. Compare the designs. What differences do you notice?

**4** Which fibres were developed between 1900 and 1960? What were they used for? Look through some magazines to find pictures that show how these fibres are used in textiles today.

**5** What was the name of the machine invented in the 1800s which allowed the textiles manufacturers to mass-produce clothing? Investigate the different types of machine available today. What are these machines able to do and how much do they cost? Identify a machine that would be suitable for the following:

    **a** a beginner

    **b** someone with lots of experience

    **c** a designer.

# The textiles industry today

The textiles industry is a global industry with large companies like Coats Viyella and Courtaulds Textiles employing many people and operating in many different countries around the world.

The use of new technology is becoming more widespread in the textiles industry. More companies are using **Computer-Aided Design (CAD), Computer-Aided Manufacture (CAM)** and **Computer Integrated Manufacture (CIM)** in the processing, designing, planning and manufacturing stages of textile products (see pages 78–9 for more information on CAD, CAM and CIM). Many companies also use hi-tech machinery.

## Textiles companies go global

Information technology has also led to changes in the textiles industry. Information in the form of words and pictures can be sent around the world by fax machine within seconds. Linked computer systems allow the user to send electronic messages from one computer to another. Computer modems, which are connected to the telephone line, allow the user to send and receive information. They also give access to the Internet and the Information Highway, enabling companies to advertise the products that they make as well as give out product information. Large amounts of data and graphics may be sent by ISDN (digital telephone lines) from one computer to another faster than is possible by modem.

## Case study

### Courtaulds Textiles

Courtaulds started in 1816 as a silk throwster (the processing and spinning of raw silk into yarn) and weaver. In 1990 it separated into two companies – Courtaulds Plc, an international chemical company, and Courtaulds Textiles Plc. Today Courtaulds Textiles is the second largest textiles and clothing company in the UK and one of the five largest in Europe.

Courtaulds supplies clothing and home furnishings to Marks & Spencer, including lingerie, underwear, nightwear, leisurewear, socks, knitwear and children's clothes.

It is the UK's largest producer of lingerie and underwear and one of the world's largest suppliers of lace and stretch fabrics.

Some of its clothing brands include Gossard, Berlei, Aristoc and Lyle & Scott.

Products of the clothing and textiles manufacturer Courtaulds Textiles: (A) children's wear, (B) underwear, (C) casual clothing

## Some of the people involved in textiles production

Fibre technologists look at ways of improving fibres and design new hi-tech ones. Textiles technologists add chemicals to improve performance of yarns. This is biotechnology.

Colourists/stylists/textiles designers create colour themes and ideas for yarn ranges.

Textiles designers produce fabric designs. Fashion designers, interior designers and accessory designers design textiles products to be sold to the consumer.

Pattern cutters create sample patterns and grade the patterns into the sizes needed.

Pattern layers use the most effective way of laying the pattern pieces on the fabric to avoid wastage. This can involve specialised machinery. Workstation teams sew the product together.

Quality control teams check that products are of correct quality.

## Questions

**1** What do the following terms mean?

  **a** CAD

  **b** CAM

  **c** CIM

**2** How do textiles companies send information quickly from one site to another?

**3** What type of company is Courtaulds Textiles? What types of textiles products does it make?

**4** What are the roles of the following people in the textiles industry?

  **a** textiles technologist

  **b** textiles designer

  **c** pattern cutter.

# Textiles and colour

*'Colour affects our life.*
*Colour is physical...we see it.*
*Colour communicates...we receive*
*information from the language of colour.*
*Colour is emotional...it evokes our feelings'.*

Source: *Colour Harmony 2* by Bride Whelan,
Thames & Hudson, 1994 (p.7)

Colour is a part of our daily lives. It is all around us and plays an essential part in the design of textiles and clothing. When choosing a textiles product, we respond first to its colour, but we may also respond to other things, such as texture and pattern.

## Colour

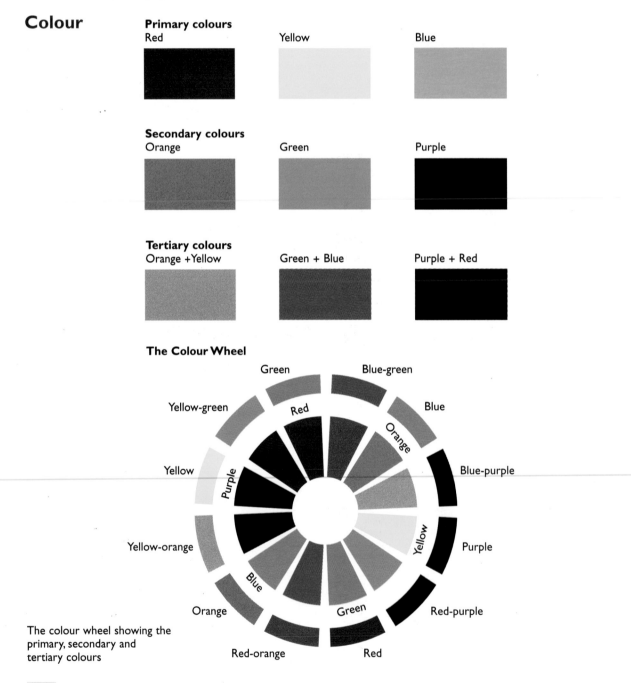

### Primary colours
Red                    Yellow              Blue

### Secondary colours
Orange             Green              Purple

### Tertiary colours
Orange +Yellow      Green + Blue       Purple + Red

### The Colour Wheel

The colour wheel showing the primary, secondary and tertiary colours

18

There are three **primary colours** or **hues**: red, yellow and blue. There are three **secondary colours**: orange, green and violet (purple). These are made by mixing together the primary colours, like this:

red + yellow = orange
yellow + blue = green
blue + red = violet (purple).

**Tertiary colours** are created by mixing a primary colour and a secondary colour, eg blue (primary colour) and green (secondary colour) may be mixed together to form blue-green.

Each of the colours at this stage is at **full saturation** or **brightness**. This means that no black, white or grey has been added. The lightness or darkness of a colour is called a **value**. Adding white to a colour makes a **tint**. Adding black to a colour makes a **shade**.

**Tone Values** (showing how white grades to black in 9 stages)
1 = White                                                                                    Black = 9

**Tints**
eg Red                                    to                        White in 5 stages

**Shades**
eg Red                                    to                        Black in 5 stages

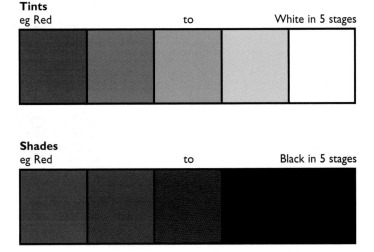

Creating tones, tints and shades

## Questions

**1** What are the primary and secondary colours? Give examples of where these colours might be used in our everyday life.

**2** How are tertiary colours made? Give some examples.

**3** What do the following terms mean: hue, brightness, value, tint, shade?

## To do

We use colour to describe everyday things, and we use descriptive words such as navy blue or bright red. Collect a range of pictures and fabrics. Arrange them in a table like the one below and then describe the colours that you see.

| Picture or fabric sample | Words that describe the colour that you can see |
|---|---|
|  |  |

# Adding colour to textiles

Many ways of adding colour to textiles have been around for a long time and some have changed very little. The time line shows the development of printed textiles from 2100BC to the present day.

## The development of printed textiles

**2100 BC** Egyptian tomb paintings show people wearing clothing with printed designs

**2000 BC** In Peru clay cylinders are used to print border prints on to fabric

**1500 BC** Tie-dye, batik, block and roller printing are developed in Mexico and Peru

**1200 BC** Batik is used in ceremonial dress. It is also developed in India, China and Java

**450 BC** In Greece animal figures are painted on to fabric using pigment dyes

**500 AD** Batik, stencil and tie dye are used widely in Japan

**1100** Fabric printing is widespread in Europe

**1200** Printed cloth is used widely in Nigeria

**1300–1600** Weaving, tapestry and silk embroidery are widespread in Europe. Printing goes into decline

**1676–1771** Printing becomes important in Europe once again, and print works are set up

**1712** The Calico Printing works are set up in North America

**1785** Industrialised roller printing is invented

**1802** A special method of printing – **the first resist method** (see below) – for mass production is developed in Britain

**1860s–80s** The British designer William Morris prints textiles and wallpaper designs in the 'art nouveau' style

**Late 1800s** Synthetic dyes developed

**1990s** A vast range of printed and dyed textiles are available in a wide range of designs influenced by cultures from all over the world.

Colour can be added:

- to the fibre before it is spun into yarn
- to the yarn before it is woven or knitted
- to the garment or the fabric when in its greige state.

There are different ways of adding colour to fabric, and these are shown below.

## Surface pattern

This involves applying a pattern to the surface of the fabric using dyes. Printed fabrics created using this method are used for clothing, home furnishings and wall-hangings. Surface pattern processes include:

screen printing; hand-block printing; roller printing; heat transfer printing; dry printing; wet printing; discharge printing; burn out printing (devoré); flock printing; warp printing (ikat).

▲ Screen printing

▶ Burn out printing uses chemicals which burn away the fabric, creating 'see-through' (sheer) and thick areas. This fabric is called devoré and is used for dresses and scarves

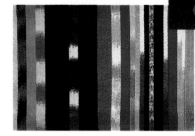

◀ Warp printing

## Dyeing and resist methods

A 'resist' such as string (tie-dye), wax (batik – from India) or starch paste (adire – from Ghana) is used to create the pattern on the fabric. The fabric is then dyed and the resist removed. This process can be repeated several times until the pattern is achieved. Yarns that are space dyed are used for knitwear and fancy embroidery threads. Dyeing and resist methods include:

tie-dye; tritik; batik; space dyeing; yarn dyeing; shibori (Japanese method of tritik); adire eleko; silk painting using gutta resists.

Tie-dye

Batik

## Surface decoration

This is the application of colour using fabrics in different ways, eg patchwork. This method can be combined with embroidery techniques, eg appliqué. Detailed surface decoration effects can be achieved by using various quilting techniques. Surface decoration methods include:

appliqué; patchwork; bead work; quilting.

Appliqué

## Embroidery

Embroidery and other methods of applying pattern have been around for many centuries. Nowadays adding colour by embroidery and other methods is mainly done by craftspeople, and a piece of work can take a long time to complete. Machine embroidery can be done on a large scale using computerised machines, and it is often used for putting designs on T-shirts and caps. Methods of embroidery include:

smocking; cross stitch; hand embroidery; machine embroidery

Machine embroidery

## Other ways of decorating fabrics

- Felting – fabrics such as wool can be felted, then embroidered
- Rag rugs – these can be made using recycled fabrics
- Tapestry – uses stitches to create pictures.

### To do

1 Gather together a range of different types of fabric or textiles products. What method of adding colour or decoration was used on each? Which method of adding colour or decoration was most used? Where would you see one method being used more than the other?

2 Choose one of the items you have looked at and make a drawing of the design that has been applied. Now redesign the pattern using a different method of applying colour or decoration. List the ways the design has changed.

# Dyeing fabrics

William Henry Perkins used the first synthetic dye in the nineteenth century. It was made from coal tars. Before this time juices of berries, plants, animals and insects were used to make dyes. For example, the Phoenicians, who lived around 1000BC on the eastern coast of the Mediterranean Sea, used a precious purple dye made from shellfish for the clothing of their kings; 12,000 shellfish were needed to make 1 g of dye.

## How is a colour decided?

Today most dyes are made from chemicals, and with so many different fibres and fabrics on the market, each requires a particular dye. The type of dye depends on the product. These are some of the questions that need to be considered:

- Does the dye suit the fibre?
- Is the dye resistant to perspiration?
- Will washing affect the dye? Is the dye **colourfast** (will not 'run' when washed)?
- Will the dye be affected by sunlight?
- Will the dye be affected by chemicals?
- Will the dye be affected by abrasion or rubbing?

Craftspeople dye their own fabrics using an industrial dye or make their own natural dyes out of leaves, bark, fruit or vegetables. A large manufacturer may use a specialist dyeing company to dye its fabrics, such as Coats Viyella Clothing – Stevensons in Derbyshire. At the same time the dyeing company will finish the fabric. This process is called dyeing and finishing.

Colours for textiles products come from many sources. In the textiles industry help on deciding colours comes from specialist trade shows and magazines. When you design or make your own products you choose the colours that are available from the materials you are using. In industry the process of creating a colour consists of three stages:

1 Stevensons' colour laboratory is given a sample of colour provided by the customer. The sample is called a pattern and in this example the customer wants to dye a cotton Lycra knitted fabric a pale orange.

Paint colour card

2 The colour is dyed in the laboratory and a sample piece of fabric made up. This is called the **colour standard,** and the information it contains is used when the colour is made up in large quantities.

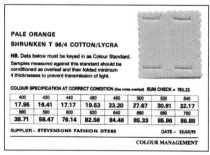

**PALE ORANGE**

**SHRUNKEN T 96/4 COTTON/LYCRA**

NB. Data below must be keyed in as Colour Standard. Samples measured against this standard should be conditioned as overleaf and then folded minimum 4 thicknesses to prevent transmission of light.

COLOUR SPECIFICATION AT CORRECT CONDITION (See notes overleaf) SUM CHECK = 783.22

| 400 | 420 | 440 | 460 | 480 | 500 | 520 | 540 |
|---|---|---|---|---|---|---|---|
| 17.95 | 16.41 | 17.17 | 19.53 | 23.20 | 27.67 | 30.61 | 32.17 |
| 560 | 580 | 600 | 620 | 640 | 660 | 680 | 700 |
| 38.71 | 68.47 | 76.14 | 82.56 | 84.46 | 85.33 | 85.96 | 86.88 |

SUPPLIER – STEVENSONS FASHION DYERS       DATE – 25/03/95

COLOUR MANAGEMENT

The colour standard

**3** Several garments made of the chosen fabric are dyed and tested to see if they match the colour standard. Once the colour passes the test it is ready for mass-production dyeing.

The final garment matches the colour standard required

## How are fabrics dyed?

When you dye your own fabrics, you will need the following information to help you. Dyes need help to be attracted to the fibres of a fabric. This is done by using a **mordant**. Vinegar is a simple mordant and can be used with animal fibres such as wool and silk. Salt is another simple mordant which can be used to help dye plant fibres like cotton and linen.

### To do

Dye fabric using the three primary colours, using your own vegetable dyes. You will need a piece of white fabric (10 x 10 cm) or yarn samples (100 g) of cotton, wool, polyester, silk

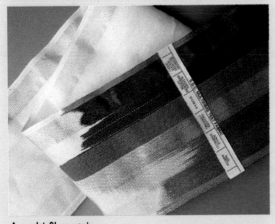

A multi-fibre strip

and linen, or you may use a **multi-fibre strip**, which is a strip of woven fabric made up of several different fibres. You should also wear protective clothing, such as gloves and aprons, and if you have long hair, tie it back.

For this experiment you will also need the following:

250 g of each vegetable dye (red = red cabbage; blue = blueberries or elderberries; yellow = onion skins or heather); containers for mixing the dyes; 2 tablespoons of salt for plant fibres or 250 ml of vinegar for animal fibres

You will need to repeat the experiment shown below three times, one for each colour that you dye.

### Method: vegetable dye

**1** Boil vegetable matter separately in 500 ml of water in a large steel or enamel saucepan for 30 minutes. Strain off and keep liquid. Divide into three equal quantities for testing with each mordant.

**2** Strain off vegetable matter saving the coloured liquid.

**3** Bring liquid to the boil again, simmer gently.

**4** Wash fabric in warm water and washing-up liquid and rinse well. Add damp fabric to liquid, add one of the mordants, then simmer for 30 minutes.

**5** Remove fabric and rinse until water turns clear.

**6** Dry fabric and note the results.

### Evaluating your results

**1** Display your dyed fabrics. What do you notice about them. Are the colours very bright ?

**2** How much did it cost to produce your dye? Compare this to the cost of buying commercial dyes, such as Dylon.

**3** Try dyeing fabrics using other dyes and compare your results.

# Equipment for textiles technology

Choosing the right tools and equipment are essential when working with textiles products, but knowing which tool or piece of equipment to use can sometimes be a problem. This is where knowledge about the product that you are making is essential. **Disassembling** (see pages 42–5) or looking at similar products and doing research will help you decide what to use.

Before using any equipment, always follow the instructions. This will ensure you get the best out of the equipment and help you to use it safely.

## The sewing machine

This piece of equipment is used to speed up the process of sewing any textiles product, and will give accurate results. It can be used to join fabrics, make buttonholes and create embroidery stitches. It can also be used to finish off a textiles product, eg hemming. Advanced sewing machines

can be linked to a computer. The computer 'sends' the design to the sewing machine which, after being programmed, will stitch the design. This is called CAD/CAM (see pages 78–9).

Some areas of the textiles industry such as **bespoke tailoring** (custom-made clothing) and **haute couture** still use traditional handsewing and hand embroidery when making up garments. Because these processes take a lot of time, only a few garments can be made and so these tend to be expensive.

A modern electric sewing machine

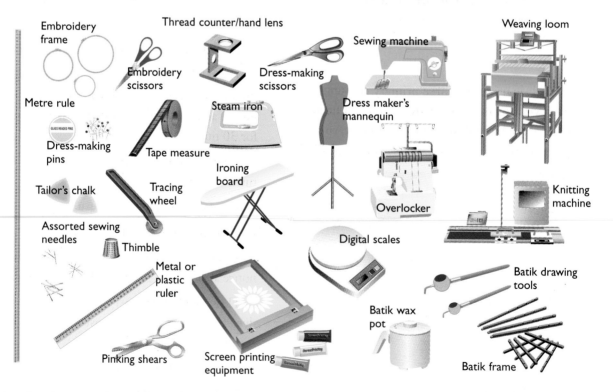

Tools and equipment used in textiles production

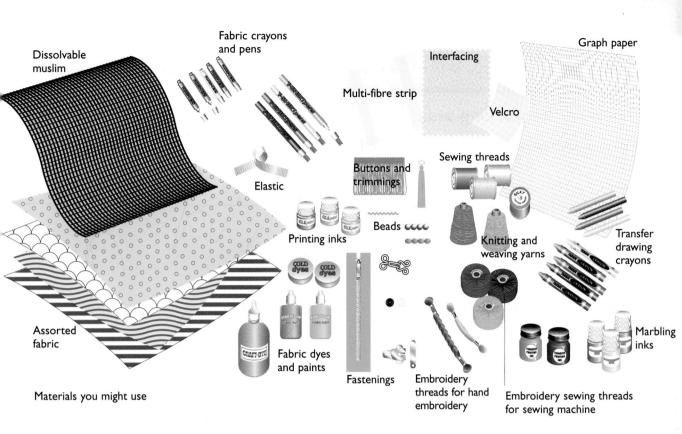

**Dissolvable muslim**

**Fabric crayons and pens**

**Interfacing**

**Graph paper**

**Multi-fibre strip**

**Velcro**

**Elastic**

**Sewing threads**

**Buttons and trimmings**

**Printing inks**

**Beads**

**Knitting and weaving yarns**

**Transfer drawing crayons**

**Assorted fabric**

**Fabric dyes and paints**

**Fastenings**

**Embroidery threads for hand embroidery**

**Embroidery sewing threads for sewing machine**

**Marbling inks**

Materials you might use

## To do

**1** Compare the results of traditional handsewing methods with the results from using a sewing machine. Look at a variety of different fabrics, then record your findings in a table like the one below. The things you need to look for are: the time it takes to complete a task, the amount of materials used, how much help you need, etc.

| Technique | Sewing machine | Handsewn | Comments |
|---|---|---|---|
| Running or back stitch | | | |
| Joining two pieces of fabric together | | | |
| Creating a buttonhole | | | |
| Sewing a small design using satin stitch | | | |

**2** Why do you think the textiles industry uses a range of different types of high-speed automated sewing machines when sewing textiles products? Give three reasons for your answer.

## Recording the results of your work

It is important to record accurately how you make your textiles product. You can do this by:

- using a 35 mm camera, camcorder or digital camera linked to a computer to take photographs at each stage of the making process
- scanning images into a computer
- using a photocopier
- using a tape recorder.

## To do

**1** Look at the photograph of the sewing machine. Describe how you might use the different attachments when sewing together different textiles products.

**2** Choose five examples of tools and equipment that can be used in your textiles technology work. Draw each item that you have chosen, then explain how and why it is used.

# Working safely with textiles

## Safety in the working area

Safety rules are given when you are working with different types of equipment to ensure that no accidents happen. Much of the equipment that you will use will have been tested by the manufacturers and will carry safety signs to say that it reached a certain safety standard.

You will also need to wear the right protective clothing when working with dyes and chemicals.

Some items of protective clothing

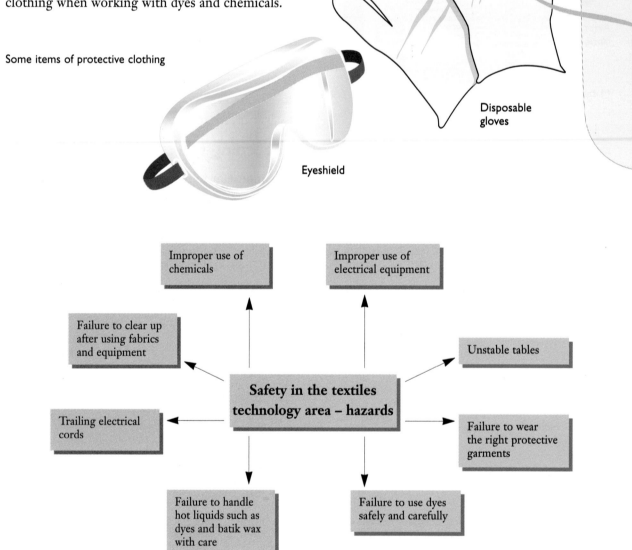

Disposable gloves

Eyeshield

Improper use of chemicals

Improper use of electrical equipment

Failure to clear up after using fabrics and equipment

Unstable tables

**Safety in the textiles technology area – hazards**

Trailing electrical cords

Failure to wear the right protective garments

Failure to handle hot liquids such as dyes and batik wax with care

Failure to use dyes safely and carefully

Hazards to watch out for when working with textiles

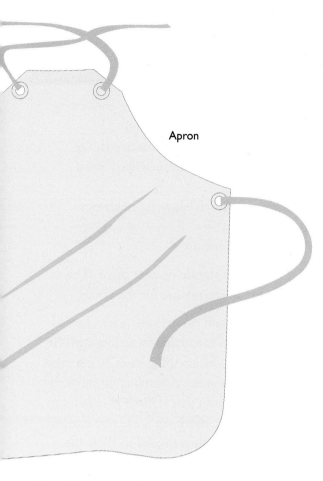

Apron

## Using electrical equipment safely

All electrical equipment for use with textiles carries some kind of warning symbol or a safety mark. Always make sure your hands are thoroughly dry before using electrical equipment, especially if you have just finished doing textiles work that involves using wet hands.

## Basic safety rules for working with textiles

1 When using equipment tie back long hair.
2 Wear proper protective clothing.
3 Make sure you know how to use the equipment you need to complete each task.
4 Check equipment before you use it. If in doubt ask your teacher.
5 Clean all equipment properly after use.
6 Always wash your hands thoroughly before leaving the textiles technology working area if you have used dyes, printing inks or any chemicals.
7 Make sure that when using equipment you work in a well-lit area.

## Making products that are safe to use

As well as looking at safety in the working area, you will also need to be aware of safety issues when making textiles products with specific end uses, eg fabrics to be used for furnishing, children's nightwear and toys. The British Standards Institution (BSI) requires that fabrics used in these ways pass a number of tests first.

Fire resistant label

### To do

**1** Choose one major piece of textiles equipment that is in use in your textiles working area, and design a guide on how to use it safely. You could use a computer program to do this.

**2** Compile a list of the types of textiles equipment in your textiles area. Give each one a rating of 1–10 using the headings below.

   **a** Ease of use – 1 = easy to use; 10 = difficult to use.

   **b** Cost to replace if broken – 1 = cheap to replace; 10 = expensive to replace.

Add two more of your own headings to the list. Display your findings.

# Costing a textiles product (1)

In industry textiles products are costed according to the number of processes that they have to go through. To this are added the cost of materials, overheads, labour costs and VAT. The manufacturer and retailer will also add on an amount to give them a profit.

## Costing a garment

An average garment goes through 9–45 steps in the making-up process. This is called the **cut, make and trim (CMT)**. It can take from three days to three weeks to get complete garments finished and in the shops. The exact time depends on the type of garment and its complexity.

The following are taken into consideration when costing a garment:

- number of components in a garment
- number of standard or straightforward operations needed

- number of non-standard or time-consuming and complex operations needed
- labour (the number of people needed to make the product)/materials/fixed costs, eg rent
- administration/overheads, eg electricity
- profit required
- VAT (value added tax).

This gives the **wholesale** or **cost price.** This is the price paid by the retailer for the goods.

The **selling** or **retail price** is the price charged in the shops and is calculated by adding a **profit margin** which can be anything from 10 per cent to 100 per cent or more, depending on the item being sold. The profit that is made is called the **gross margin.** The **mark-up** is the percentage of the cost price which is needed to allow the retailer to get the selling price and make a profit.

Machinist sewing a garment

**Pricing a garment**

Let's look at how the price of a summer dress made from viscose rayon is worked out.

The selling price is £20.99

The cost of making the dress is £8.99

The retailer's profit is calculated as £20.99 - £8.99

Profit = £12

Gross margin = £12.00 ÷ £20.99 x 100 = 57.17%

Mark-up = profit ÷ cost price x 100

£12 ÷ £8.99 x 100 = 133.48%

To achieve a profit on the dress the retailer's mark-up is 133.48%

## To do

Work out the profit, the gross margin and the percentage mark-up on each of the following textiles products for the retailer:

a  a pair of trainers – cost price £12.50, selling price £75.00

b  a single-bed duvet cover – cost price £5.50, selling price £28.99

c  a 50/50% wool cashmere winter coat – cost price £55.00, selling price £350

d  a 100% polyester chiffon printed scarf – cost price £0.95, selling price £10.99

## Added value

The selling price of a garment can be increased if it has lots of additional or special features or is made with a certain type of fibre. This is called giving the garment 'added value'.

Retailers also try to give the impression of value for money by selling goods at a certain price like £9.99 or £15.99. This type of pricing helps to make customers think they are getting a bargain.

## To do

**1** Choose a textiles product and try to work out the number of stages you think it took to make the product. Start by listing the fabrics the product is made from and the types of fastenings used and so on. Make a flowchart of the stages to help you. Remember, the more stages there are and the better the quality of the materials used, the more expensive the product is likely to be.

**2** a  Choose an item of clothing that you wear. Note down all the components needed to make it, eg numbers of zips and buttons and the approximate amount of fabric used.

b  Work out how much it would cost you to make the garment if you had bought all the components yourself. Use a specialist sewing catalogue or visit a local shop to find out prices.

c  What is the difference in cost between making it yourself or buying it from a shop? Do your findings surprise you? Give two reasons for your answer.

# Costing a textiles product (2)

Case study

**Costing a range of printed fabrics for mass production**

Manufacturers need to consider a number of costs when working out the total cost of producing a textiles product on a large scale. For example, to work out the cost of producing a range of printed fabrics the manufacturer will need to include:

- the cost of the base fabric – this is the fabric in its greige state or finished state (see pages 50–51 for information on finishes)
- the cost of materials – dyes, inks, chemicals, printing equipment
- the cost of design – the time taken to design the fabric and colourways
- the cost of conversion (making the yarn into fabric) – this includes the manufacturer's overheads, such as rent, lighting and wages.

## Costing your own textiles product

One of the things that you will need to do before making a textiles product is to work out how much it will cost to produce. This cost will depend on the type of product and the quality and number of components it uses. First, you need to decide what items you will have to buy to make up your product.

You will need to add up the cost of the individual items to find the total cost of making your product.

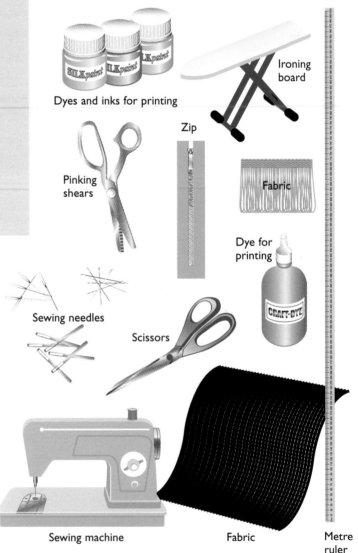

Dyes and inks for printing · Ironing board · Pinking shears · Zip · Fabric · Dye for printing · Sewing needles · Scissors · Iron · Buttons · Trimmings · Threads · Sewing machine · Fabric · Metre ruler

Items that might be needed to make up textiles products

### Working out the cost of a plain 'A' line skirt

To work out the total cost of making the skirt, add together the costs in the final column of the chart:

£4.49 + £0.55 + £0.79 + £0.25 + £2.50 = £8.58

This does not include the time you took to make the skirt – your labour – or the cost of overheads, eg the cost of operating your sewing machine. You would only need to consider these if you were going to sell your product.

| Item | Amount | Cost per metre/item | Total cost |
|---|---|---|---|
| Printed 100% cotton fabric | 1.5 metres (115 cm wide) | £2.99 per metre | £4.49 |
| Firm iron-on interfacing | 0.5 metres (90 cm wide) | £1.10 per metre | £0.55 |
| Metal zip | 1 x 14 cm long | £0.79 | £0.79 |
| Button | 1 x 15 mm button | £0.25 | £0.25 |
| Cotton sewing thread | 2 x 1000-metre reels | £1.25 | £2.50 |

**1** You have been asked to find out the cost of making the doll shown in the commercial pattern (a pattern you can buy in a shop). The items needed to make the doll are shown below. Use a sewing catalogue or visit a local specialist shop to help you.

0.7 m of 115 cm wide 100% plain cotton fabric, 105 g polyester stuffing, 0.2 m wool yarn
Fine point non-toxic fabric marker, 0.3 m of 3–6 mm wide ribbon

**2** Work out how much it would cost to produce:

    **a** 10 dolls **b** 50 dolls **c** 100 dolls **d** 500 dolls.
You could use a computer spreadsheet program
to help you.

**3** If it took you 2 hours to make the doll and you included your labour at £3.50 an hour, how much would it cost you to make?

Pattern for a soft toy

# Designing a textiles product

## What is textiles design?

Textiles design is about designing all types of fabrics by adding colour, texture and pattern for a particular customer for a particular end use. The person who designs these products is called a **textiles designer.**

Woven fabrics by designer Annie Black

Printed fabric by print designer Linda Nottingham

Knitted fabrics by knitwear designer Rose Sinclair

## What is a design brief?

A **design brief** is a short statement of the task to be solved. It is sometimes called a **design proposal.** It may contain information about the type of people that the product is aimed at, the existing product range and any improvements that may need to be made to a new product before it can be produced. A design brief might include the following information:

- the types of fibre, yarn and fabric to be used
- the purpose of the design
- the sort of climate that the product will be used in and the activity it will be used for
- the price range for the product
- the type of decoration
- the number of colours/pattern repeats
- the age group the product is aimed at.

 Single motif

 Block repeat. Pattern is repeated identically

 Brick repeat

 Half drop repeat. Pattern is moved half-way down along side previous pattern

Different ways of printing a pattern repeat

The designer then produces a range of designs to fit the design brief. If these do not match the market that the product is aimed at, the designer **modifies** the designs or produces new ones.

The design brief is written

Marketing and research take place

A **storyboard** is produced. It displays the designer's initial ideas

A range of working drawings is produced, and initial costings are done

First sample of fibre, yarn, fabric, garment or accessory is produced. It is then modified and a second (production) sample is made.

Further costings are done and specifications for all aspects of production are drawn up

Stages in the design process

At each stage in the design process people from the marketing, sales, technical and production departments are involved. They work together with the designer as a team.

Once the design process is complete, the designs are looked at again to make sure that they match the design brief. They are then shown at a formal presentation to the company that set the brief. The company decides whether to go ahead with the final designs.

## Questions

**1** What is a design brief? How is it used by the designer?

**2** What are the stages in producing a design brief? Make a list.

**3** Why does the designer work with the marketing, sales and technical teams when a design is being developed? Give three reasons for your answer.

**4** Textiles designers design a range of products both for interiors (in homes) and for fashion clothing. Zandra Rhodes is a textiles designer famous for her hand-painted and hand-printed garments. What can you find out about any other famous textiles designers and the work they produce?

## What is a design specification?

A **design specification** gives details about the design of the textiles product being made. The design specification must meet the brief. For example, this is the sort of information that a specification for designing a range of printed fabrics could include:

- the number of colours in the print design
- the number of colourways for each design
- whether the design needs to be in repeat
- the type of printing method to be used
- any special effects needed

- the types of fibre and fabric to be used
- the number of sample fabric swatches if required
- initial costings.

Only after the final designs have been accepted is a more detailed specification drawn up (see pages 36–7).

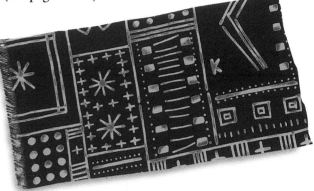

A swatch is a small piece of finished fabric design. The size varies depending on whether the fabric is knitted, woven or printed, eg a swatch of knitted fabric is 30 x 30 cm

### To do

Make a list of the key words in the design briefs shown below. Then make a second list showing a range of ideas that could be suitable for each brief.

**a** Design a range of socks suitable for 5–8-year-olds. The socks must contain cotton as the main fibre, and must use cartoon characters as their main design theme.

**b** Design a range of clothing suitable for a group of teenagers aged 14–18 years for a camping trip that is to take place from September to October on Dartmoor in south-west England. It must be warm but allow the skin to breathe. It must also be waterproof, yet fashionable.

**c** Design a range of hats for both male and females of any age group that are suitable to wear in the winter months. The hats must be fashionable.

# Analysing a design brief

Now let's look at two examples of design briefs:

1 'To design a collection of printed fashion fabrics suitable for a range of summer clothing for 14–18-year-old girls. The colours and the fabrics used should be in line with the trends predicted for Spring/Summer '98/99.'

A year or season guide is always given, such as Spring/Summer '96 or Autumn /Winter '96/97, as fabric designers usually work 12–18 months in advance of the season they are designing for.

2 'To design a range of summer waistcoats to complement an existing range of "active clothing" aimed at the 11–14 years age group. The waistcoats should incorporate the company logo.'

The next step is to **analyse** the design brief. You do this by picking out the key words. The key words in the first design brief are *printed, fashion fabrics, summer clothing, 14–18-year-olds, trends* for *Spring/Summer '98*. In industry the designer would be expected to produce at least six different ideas for fabrics with three or four **colourways** for each design. Colourways are the same design

LADIES SWEATER

Examples of colourways – knitted garment by Shima Seiki

shown in different colours. The designer might also show how the fabric would look in garment form. He or she would use a range of drawing skills as well as Computer-Aided Design (CAD) software (see pages 78–9) to produce the designs.

The key words in the second design brief are *summer waistcoats, complement, active clothing, 11–14 years, company logo*. Here the designer will have been given a range of fabrics and examples of clothing with logos. He or she would be expected to design 15–20 working drawings showing exactly what the garments would look like. The designer would use fashion-drawing skills and a CAD software database on which templates for different fashion poses and garment components such as pockets are stored.

## Gathering information for design proposals

Let's say you are designing a range of printed fabrics. Here is the research that you might do:

- Collect pictures from books and magazines or postcards on a theme, eg geometric shapes. You would then pick out key colours and shapes and create a storyboard to develop your designs.
- Visit shops to look at what is being sold.
- Collect a range of pictures from specialist fashion magazines.
- Visit museums with garment and textiles areas.
- Produce a questionnaire and do a survey of a number of people at whom the product is to be aimed to find out what they like to wear.
- Collect a range of printed fabrics that show current trends.
- Ask experts such as textiles designers, fashion designers and fashion buyers for ideas.

And sweet it was to fancy
that even the blackest ground
was proud of its single daisy
rooted in bitter ground.

Examples of storyboards

## To do

Using a variety of information, create a storyboard which will show ideas, colours and themes on one of the topics listed below.

**a** a new range of socks aimed at 11–16-year-olds

**b** a new range of sportswear for snowboarding

**c** a new range of clothing for 3–5-year-olds based on a cartoon character

**d** a new range of fabrics suitable for summer dresses for 11–14-year-olds

**e** a new range of fabrics for the interior or foyer of a public building such as a school, theatre or library

**f** a new range of fabrics and coordinated wallpapers based on the theme of either the paintings and drawings of Leonardo da Vinci or a well-known cartoon character or characters from a novel.

# Writing a specification for a textiles product

Before any textiles product can be put into full-scale production, an exact set of details about the product needs to be written. These details are called **specifications**. They lay down a set of standards about the product which must be maintained throughout every stage of production.

Some parts of the specification will be fixed, eg what the colour of the product is to be. Other parts indicate the **parameters** or **tolerances** (limits) within which the manufacturer may work, eg the length of a skirt may be set at 30 cm with a tolerance of 1.5 cm, so a skirt length measuring 28.5 cm or 31.5 cm would be acceptable. But a skirt measuring 28 cm or 32 cm would be unacceptable.

Before a specification can be written, tests are carried out to ensure that the textiles product being produced meets certain standards. Once all the tests have been successfully carried out, the company issuing the design brief will then agree that the specification standards are what it requires. The manufacturer of the product will work to these specifications and will continue to test at each stage of production to make sure that all the items being made are of the same quality.

A specification is always checked thoroughly before being sent to the production line. Because a textiles product might be designed, cut out and made up in different places it is important to have a specification to check for faults. When writing a specification you need to make sure that you can use it to make an accurate copy of your design, as well as check each stage of the making up process to make sure your product is correct and there are no faults.

The main specifications used in the textiles industry are:

- **fabric specification** – includes all the information needed about the fabric before it is cut out
- **product specification** – includes details of what the finished product should be like and all the things that need to be done to make it
- **manufacturing specification** – lists the number of operations needed to make a product and the processes to take place
- **garment specification** – includes all the things needed to make up the garment before production.

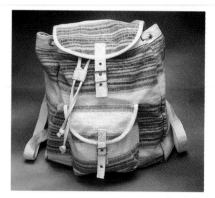

Photograph A

Photograph B

| Fabric specification | Product specification | Manufacturing specification | Garment specification |
| --- | --- | --- | --- |
| Type of fabric | Description of the product to be made | Name of manufacturing process | Drawing of the outfit or styles to be made |
| Fibre content | Illustrations of the final drawings | Materials to be used, including fabric type, measurements, shade | Description of which fabrics should be made up into a particular style |
| Amount of fabric | Fabric amounts | Type of thread to be used | Number of trims or components needed |
| Fabric length | Trims | Machines used to sew garment from start to finish | Set of patterns in all the sizes that the garments will be made into |
| Width and weight | Measurements | | |
| **Picks** and **ends** per cm (**Ends** are the number of **warp** or vertical threads in a centimetre of woven fabric; **picks** are the number of **weft** or horizontal threads. These set the fineness of the fabric and its end use) | Stitch types | Stitch type | Garment dimensions and key measurements |
| | Seam types | Needle size | |
| | Instructions for putting together | Maximum stitching speed | A separate specification is needed of the stitch and seams that will be used on the garment |
| | Description of the machines to be used | Tools | |
| | | Method of making a quality product | Details of the process and machinery to be used |
| Weave structure (plain, twill, etc.) | | | |
| Shrinkage | | | |
| Shade | | | |
| Surface properties (whether or not the fabric has been finished) | | | |

What each specification contains

# Design ideas and getting information

There are many things to think about when designing a textiles product:

- Does it fulfil a need? If so, what need, eg to give warmth?
- Is there a market for the product?
- Current trends in lifestyle, social trends, cultural trends, economic trends.
- Influences on lifestyles, eg music, film, media, information technology.
- Has something similar been done before, and has it been successful? Who did it and when? Can you make a product just as good, or better?
- Costs of designs, manufacturing and labour.
- Can the designs be produced on the machines available? These are called the **production parameters**.

- What is the design specification of the product?
- How will you make sure the product is of the correct quality?
- What colours are to be used?
- Will new skills or techniques be needed in the manufacturing process?
- Are new fibres, yarns or fabrics to be used?

## Getting ideas and information

Information for your ideas can come from different sources. Information that you gather is called **research**. There are two types of research:

- **Primary research** involves gathering information to find out more about a particular project, eg asking for people's views about a product through questionnaires and interviews.
- **Secondary research** involves gathering information that is already available, eg from books, newspapers, magazines, libraries, etc.

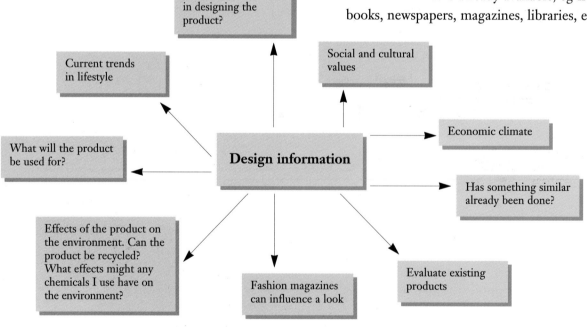

The information you will need when you start to design

The textiles industry uses research so as to keep up with trends and to predict what the next range of products will be. Without research it is difficult to develop a whole range of ideas.

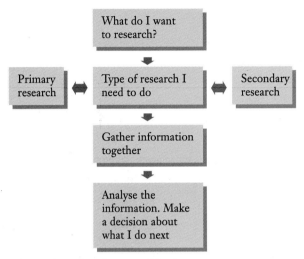

Why do I need to do research?

## Putting your ideas on paper

First, you should note down what information you need. You can put your ideas in a sketchbook, on design sheets or create **mood, theme** or **trend boards** (see pages 40–41). You will also need to analyse the information that you have gathered and make decisions on how to use it. This may involve producing a questionnaire and presenting your results. This will enable you to decide what to do next, as well as provide you with a list of further information or the type of equipment you need.

### To do

**1** In order to create a new range of T-shirts that reflect the type of music that appeals to teenagers a design company needs to know:

   **a** how much teenagers spend on T-shirts

   **b** the fabrics that their T-shirts are made of

   **c** the most popular images on T-shirts

   **d** the most popular types of music.

Research this information. Present your results. What would be the next thing you would do? Give two reasons.

**2** Using some of the information you gathered create a range of designs for the T-shirts. You could use a computer drawing or paint program to create your designs. What other information would you need before you could make a sample T-shirt?

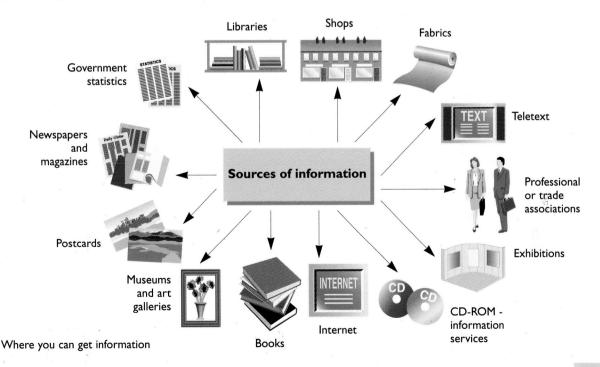

Where you can get information

# Displaying design ideas

Sketching out your design ideas is one way of showing how your ideas have developed, and can be used to describe what you have done. Good presentation of your work is very important. Initial ideas can be sketched on paper, then scanned into a computer drawing or painting program, or ideas can be drawn straight on to the computer using a graphics tablet (a large pad) with a stylus that works just like a pen or pencil. You can use other types of computer peripherals such as digital cameras (see pages 76–79 for more information).

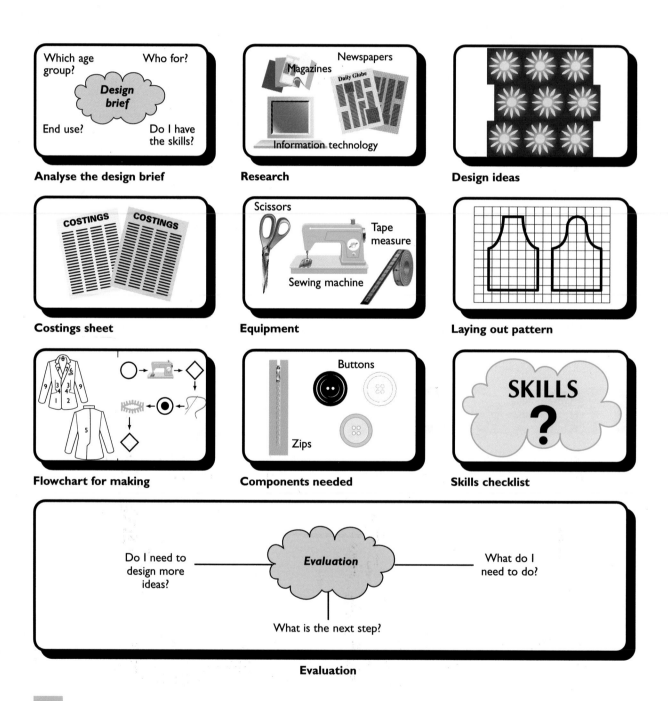

**Analyse the design brief**

**Research**

**Design ideas**

**Costings sheet**

**Equipment**

**Laying out pattern**

**Flowchart for making**

**Components needed**

**Skills checklist**

**Evaluation**

## Creating a mood board

Designers often use **mood** or **image boards** to show their ideas. Mood boards can also help you to develop your design ideas and to define the market that you are designing for.

Mood boards may show:
- yarn ideas for fabrics
- trends and ideas using different types of fabrics
- pictures and images of a particular lifestyle
- a display of different trimmings and braids
- a range of pictures inspiring your ideas.

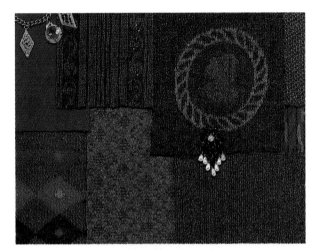

Mood board showing fabric designs and ideas

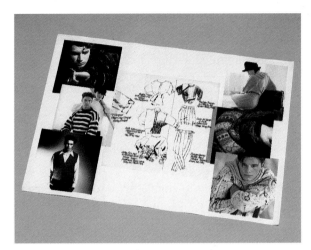

Mood board showing clothing ideas and designs

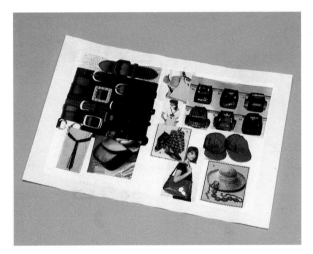

Mood board showing accessory ideas. They can be shown on their own or teamed together with other items of clothing

Mood board showing ideas for furnishing fabrics. These can be shown in room settings. This may be done using a 3-D computer program

### To do

**1** Create a series of four mood boards to reflect the colours of spring, summer, autumn and winter. They should show the use of knitwear throughout each of these seasons. The boards should be no larger than an A3 size sheet of paper and no smaller than A4. Present your finished mood boards with text explaining why you have chosen the images and colours on your boards.

**2** Create your own initial ideas sheet and mood boards based on one of the following:
- fabrics
- clothing
- furnishing fabrics
- accessories.

# Disassembling textiles products

By looking at and touching a textiles product you can find out certain things about it. For example, how many colours does it use? Does it feel rough or smooth or is it hard or soft? What is its thickness – can you see through the product when you hold it up to the light? Does the fabric stretch?

To understand more clearly how a textiles product is made up, it has to be taken apart, or **disassembled.** This process is sometimes called **deconstruction,** and can take place at any stage of the manufacturing process. Manufacturers also use disassembling to enable them to recycle parts of a product for later use.

The chart shows the kind of information that you might find out by disassembling a textiles product.

Textiles companies disassemble products:
- to assess an existing product
- to produce a specification for a new product
- to look at products of the past, and update them for today's use
- to correct faults that might occur at any point in the manufacturing process
- to ensure products are of the correct quality
- to look at ways in which a product might be reused or recycled to help protect the environment.

**Care labels** attached by manufacturers to textiles products to help us look after the things that we buy can sometimes give us added information when disassembling a product.

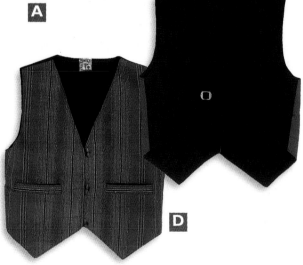

## To do

**1** Look at photos A–D. For each textiles product, make a list of five things that you can find out by looking at the product.

**2** Make a second list of five more things you could find out about the product if you had it in front of you.

**3** Choose one of the products and draw four different designs from the one shown. List the changes you made to the original design and give your reasons.

| Textile | Name of Textile | Information |
|---------|-----------------|-------------|
| | **Yarns / threads** | Fibre content; fibre length; yarn count (the thickness of a yarn); yarn twist; suggested end use, eg sewing, knitting, weaving; faults, eg knots; colours; dyes used, eg synthetic or natural dyes |
| | **Felted / non-woven fabric** | Fibre content; fibre length; fabric weight; colour/dyes used; suggested end use, eg clothing such as hats, disposable cloths, medical uses |
| | **Woven fabric** | Fibre content, fibre length, yarn count, fabric weight; fabric construction techniques, eg type of weave; colours used; suggested end use, eg garments, furnishing fabrics; any surface pattern added; surface texture; weight of fabric |
| | **Knitted fabric** | Fibre content; yarn count; yarn twist; fabric weight; construction technique; type of machine used; type of stitch formation (pattern); colours used; suggested end use, eg clothing, furnishing fabrics; surface texture |
| | **Printed and dyed fabric** | Yarn count; fibre content, number of colours; print pattern repeat; possible dyeing/print method used; suggested end use eg clothing, furnishings; type of dye or print medium used; knitted or woven; weight of the fabric. |
| | **Accessories, eg footwear, bags, umbrellas** | Fibre and yarn content; colours; type of fabric; method of construction; suggested end use; number of pieces (components) needed to make item; types of finishing and fastenings |
| | **Indoor and outdoor clothing** | Number of components in garment; amount of thread needed to complete garment; number of notions/fastenings used (eg buttons, zips); types of trims used; type of decoration and method of application size of garment; types of seam used |

Information gained from disassembling different textiles products

# Disassembling ties

Ties are worn by people of all ages either as part of school uniform or work uniform. Men also wear them to give a smart appearance with a jacket or suit. Ties are also called fashion accessories. They come in all shapes and sizes and can be made from a wide range of fabrics. The designs vary from stripes to cartoon patterns to geometric shapes. Almost any type of pattern can be woven or printed on to a tie.

A range of ties

## Things to look for when disassembling a tie

Before starting to **disassemble** (take apart) a tie you need to measure the width and length, as the longer and wider a tie is the more expensive it will be. As you disassemble the tie, you should think about the following:

- Is it a traditional or fashionable tie?
- What is its fibre content, eg silk, polyester?
- What type of weave has been used for the fabric, eg twill, satin, jacquard?
- What type of printing/dyeing method has been used?
- What colours does the tie use?
- What type of design does it use, eg geometric shapes, cartoon characters, etc?
- What is the shape of the tie? Is it narrow or wide, linear or bottle-shaped?
- Does it have a care label? Does the label give the name of the manufacturer or retailer?

You also need to think about the type of customer the tie was aimed at, including the customer's age group and the tie's price bracket. You should note, if possible, how the tie was packaged, eg in a plastic/cellophane sleeve, presentation wallet.

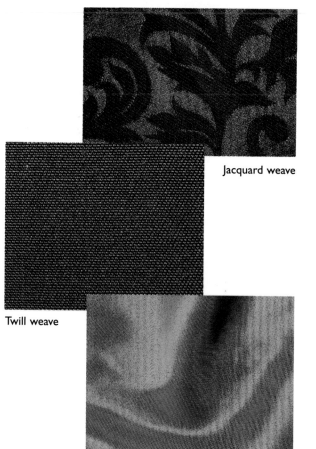

Jacquard weave

Twill weave

Satin weave

**1** Research the range of ties currently available on the market. You may need to visit specialist tie shops and use magazines to help you. Pay particular attention to the design features, colours, cost and type of fabric used, as well as the fibre content. Do you notice any differences? You could also look at ties that friends or relatives may have. Using old photographs can help you to see how tie styles have changed.

**2** You will need the following equipment to help you with this exercise: sharp pair of scissors, stitch unpicker, digital weighing scales, ruler, tape measure, magnifying glass or hand lens.

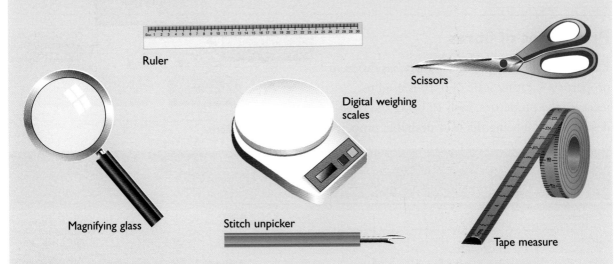

Ruler

Scissors

Digital weighing scales

Magnifying glass

Stitch unpicker

Tape measure

Equipment for disassembling a textiles product

**a** Disassemble very carefully a range of ties. Note the components and try to estimate the number of stages needed to construct the tie.

**b** As a class evaluate your findings. Display your results. You could use a computer to do this, eg use a database to store the information you found, a spreadsheet program to present your findings and word-processing software to write up your results.

**3** Design a range of ties. Choose your market from the choices below:

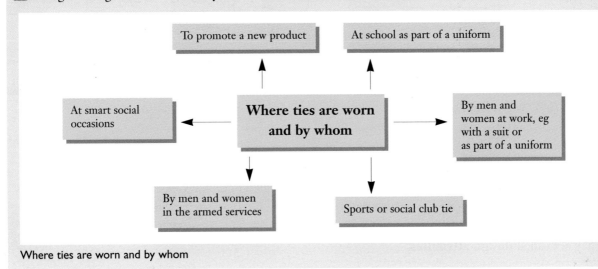

To promote a new product

At school as part of a uniform

At smart social occasions

**Where ties are worn and by whom**

By men and women at work, eg with a suit or as part of a uniform

By men and women in the armed services

Sports or social club tie

Where ties are worn and by whom

# Properties of textiles

Different fibres have different **properties** or **characteristics.** These make them suitable for different jobs. The properties of fibres are improved when the fibres are spun into yarn and can be improved further when the yarn is made into fabric.

## Properties of fibres

Each of the fibres listed in the chart has different properties. A rating scale of 0–10 is used to measure the properties, with 10 being the most desirable and 0 being the least desirable property.

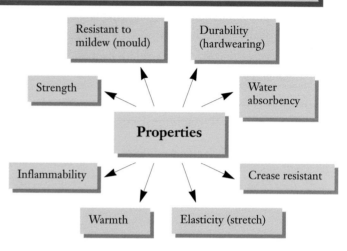

Properties of fibres

| | Durability | Strength | Flammability | Warmth | Elasticity | Crease resistant | Resistant to mildew | Water absorbency |
|---|---|---|---|---|---|---|---|---|
| Cotton | 10 | 8 | 1 | 5 | 8 | 1 | 1 | 10 |
| Linen | 10 | 10 | 1 | 5 | 0 | 0 | 1 | 10 |
| Silk | 10 | 8 | 5 | 8 | 8 | 5 | 1 | 10 |
| Wool | 1 | 1 | 5 | 10 | 10 | 10 | 5 | 10 |
| Acrylic | 5 | 8 | 1 | 10 | 10 | 10 | 10 | 5 |
| Nylon | 10 | 10 | 8 | 0 | 10 | 8 | 10 | 0 |
| Polyester | 10 | 10 | 8 | 1 | 8 | 10 | 10 | 0 |
| Rayon | 1 | 5 | 1 | 0 | 0 | 10 | 3 | 8 |
| Viscose | 1 | 5 | 10 | 0 | 1 | 1 | 2 | 10 |
| Acetate | 1 | 5 | 5 | 1 | 5 | 5 | 5 | 8 |
| Elastane (Lycra) | 10 | 5 | 1 | 1 | 10 | 10 | 10 | 1 |

Properties of fibres

Other headings that can be used in rating fibres and their properties are windproof, water repellancy and ease of washing. All of these properties are measurable, but there are other types of properties that are not so easy to measure – these are the aesthetic (visual) and tactile (feel) properties such as drape and texture. They are called **design attributes.**

Different fibres can be mixed or blended together to create a more versatile fabric, eg cotton Lycra, which is used in leggings, or polyester cotton, which is used in shirts and bedding. You can use a star profile to assess the quality of the fabric, or its fibre content.

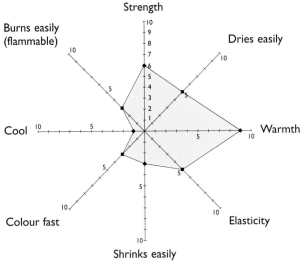

Strength

Burns easily
(flammable)

Dries easily

Cool

Warmth

Colour fast

Elasticity

Shrinks easily

A star profile

## Questions

Look at the chart showing fibre properties and answer the questions below:

a   Which fibre scored the highest? You will need to total the scores for each fibre.

b   Is it the best all-round fibre?

c   What can be done to improve fabrics that scored well in some properties but less well in others?

d   Which fibre scored the lowest? Why do you think this is?

## To do

**1** Look at photos A–E. List the properties that the fabrics used for each of the products would need to have. Suggest suitable fabrics for each product.

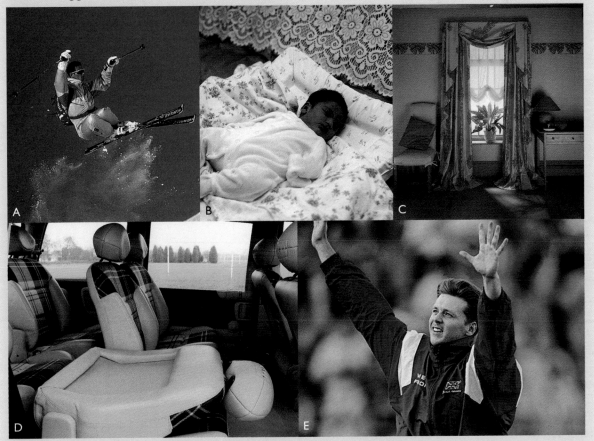

A

B

C

D

E

**2** Using the chart on the properties of fibres, list the warmest fibre and the coolest. Give your reasons. Which fibre has the greatest degree of absorbency and which the lowest rate? Give your reasons.

# Testing fabrics

Fabrics are tested to ensure that they can do the job that is intended. In industry products are tested at each stage of the production and manufacturing processes to make sure that they match the specifications that have been set. Here are some of the tests that may be carried out on textiles products:

fabric weight; warmth; water absorbency; shrinkage; durability; dyefastness; strength; elasticity; flammability; crease recovery.

## To do

Test a range of fabrics for their warmth properties. *You will need to use boiling water when you carry out this experiment. You should wear protective clothing. Be very careful and only carry out the test under the supervision of a teacher.*

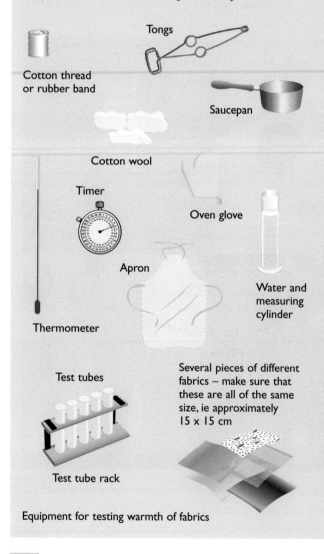

Cotton thread or rubber band

Tongs

Saucepan

Cotton wool

Timer

Oven glove

Apron

Water and measuring cylinder

Thermometer

Test tubes

Several pieces of different fabrics – make sure that these are all of the same size, ie approximately 15 x 15 cm

Test tube rack

Equipment for testing warmth of fabrics

## Method

Before you begin use a measuring cylinder to check how much water a test tube will hold. This will be the amount of water that will be needed for each test tube.

**1** Wrap a piece of fabric round a test tube, making sure the bottom is covered. Secure the fabric with cotton thread or a rubber band. Do this for each of the fabrics you are testing. Place the test tubes in the rack.

**2** Heat water in a saucepan to boiling point (100 °C). Wearing an oven glove, use a thermometer to check this.

**3** Pour the water into a measuring cylinder. Using the tongs to hold the measuring cylinder, put the correct amount of water into each test tube and insert a thermometer in each. Seal the top of the test tubes with cotton wool.

**4** Measure the temperature in each test tube after 1 minute and again at 5, 10, 15 and 20 minutes. Note down your results.

### Evaluating your results

**1** Which fabrics kept water the warmest for the longest time?

**2** Rank your results in order. Put the fabrics with the greatest warmth properties first.

**3** What does the information you have gathered show you? How do you think you could use this information in your work?

## Weight of fabric

It is important to test how heavy or light a fabric is because this is one of the things that can help you decide whether a fabric is suitable for its end use. You can find out this information by feeling the fabric but a more accurate method is to weigh the fabric.

## Warmth

Some fabrics are needed to keep people warm in cold climates, others are needed to keep people cool in hot climates.

## Water absorbency

As fabric gets wet, water is trapped between the fibres, causing the water to be absorbed. Some fabrics absorb more water than others. The end use of some fabrics such as towelling means that they must be able to absorb water.

## Shrinkage

Fabrics may either be washed by hand, machine laundered or dry-cleaned. It is important to know how a fabric will react when water is added, for if a fabric shrinks this may cause problems.

## Durability

Some fabrics need to be hardwearing (durable), eg those that are used for suitcases, since they are often used to carry heavy loads, or for garments that undergo a lot of wear and tear like overalls.

## Dyefastness

Some textiles products are tested for their dyefastness or colourfastness. It is important that dyes do not run when the products are being laundered because this can be considered a fault.

## Strength

The end use of some textiles products means that they have to be very strong, eg the webbing used in car-seat belts or clothing used in outdoor sportswear.

## Elasticity

Elasticity in fabrics used for clothing can give added comfort. This type of fabric is used in sportswear and in garments that are required to have a certain amount of 'give'.

## Crease recovery

When textiles products such as garments are transported they are likely to get crushed so it is important that the fabrics they are made of are able to recover from creasing. When a garment is pressed, the creases must iron out with ease. One of the ways that a fabric loses its shape is when it creases. If a fabric does not recover from creasing it will not look good.

## Flammability

It is essential to know how fabrics will act when they burn, as fabrics are used for many garments and as furnishing materials. Many fabrics used in furnishing are treated to help to stop them burning. The **British Standards Institution (BSI)** lays down strict guidelines on the way fabrics should be produced and used in certain goods. You will find low flammability labels on furniture and on children's nightdresses.

**LOW FLAMMABILITY
TO BS 5722
AND IS 148**

**FLAME RETARDANT
FINISH**

Low flammability label on a child's nightdress

*Further fabric tests and information about testing may be found in the Teacher's Resource Pack.*

# Adding a finish to fabrics

A **finish** may be added to a fabric to enable it to do a particular job. For example, children's nightdresses are given a flame retardant finish to make them less flammable. Finishes are usually added after the weaving or knitted stage of the manufacturing process, but it is possible to coat fibres with finishes before they are spun and made into fabric.

The type of finish that is given to a textiles product will be decided at the design brief stage and will be costed into the final product. This is called giving a product 'added value', which means that it can be sold at a higher price than a similar product without the finish. Adding a finish to the fabric can improve the appearance and the properties. For example, adding a stain resist finish such as Teflon to a cotton or wool knitted fabric not only makes the fabric easy to clean but also gives two added advantages: it prevents 'pilling' (little bobbles on the surface of the fabric) and also the loss of colour when the fabric is washed, which means the garment will keep its 'new' appearance for longer.

| Finish | Fibres it can be used on | End products |
|---|---|---|
| Flameproof | Cotton, wool | Clothing, furnishings |
| Waterproof | Cotton, wool, silk, linen | Clothing, outdoor tents |
| Stain resistant | Most fibre types | Clothing, household furnishings |
| Crease resistant | Cotton, linen, viscose, rayon | Clothing |
| Mothproof | Wool | Clothing, carpets |
| Resistant to bacteria | Cotton, linen | Shower curtains |
| Anti-static | Synthetic fibres | Underwear |
| Shrink resistant | Cotton, wool | Clothing |
| Strengthening | Cotton | Clothing, outdoor wear |
| Stiffening | Cotton | Clothing, some accessories |
| Permanent press | Synthetic fibres, wool | Clothing |
| Coolness | Synthetic fibres, cotton blends | Sportswear |
| Windproof | Cotton, wool | Clothing |

Types of finish

## Types of finish

Finishes can be applied to fabrics:

- to improve their look and feel, eg napping/brushing, which raises the surface of the fabric to give it a warm look and feel
- to increase the life of the fabric, eg mothproofing
- to improve the wear of the fabric, eg a crease resistant finish.

Finishes are usually shown on 'swing' tickets attached to the textiles product. These tell the customer that the product has extra value added to it in the form of a hi-tech finish.

A swing ticket gives extra information about the product you are buying, eg whether it has any special finishes or features. It is sometimes called informative labelling or advertising

**1** Which finishes would you use on the following products?
- **a** children's nightdresses
- **b** covering for a settee
- **c** range of clothing for a hike in the country
- **d** carpet for a child's playroom.

**a** Child's nightie

**b** Sofa covered in fabric

**c** Range of clothing for a hike, eg walking shoes, waterproof jacket and trousers, jumper

**d** Carpet (plain, brightly coloured, hardwearing)

**2** Give three reasons why manufacturers add finishes to fabrics.

**3** Which types of finishes are used on:
- **a** all types of fabrics
- **b** natural fibres only
- **c** synthetic fibres only
- **d** regenerated fibres only?

**4** Which finishes are suitable for:
- **a** clothing
- **b** underwear
- **c** outerwear
- **d** household goods
- **e** accessories?

# Labelling textiles products

Because of the many ways in which textiles products are used and the different fibres and fabrics used to make them, they need to be cared for and laundered in different ways. For example, woollen jumpers felt up if washed in a hot wash unless they have been treated for shrinkage. The information that you need to care for your textiles products is usually found on the **care label** that is attached to the product.

## What information is on the care label?

The information on a care label varies depending on the textile product. The examples below show you the type of information that might appear on a care label.

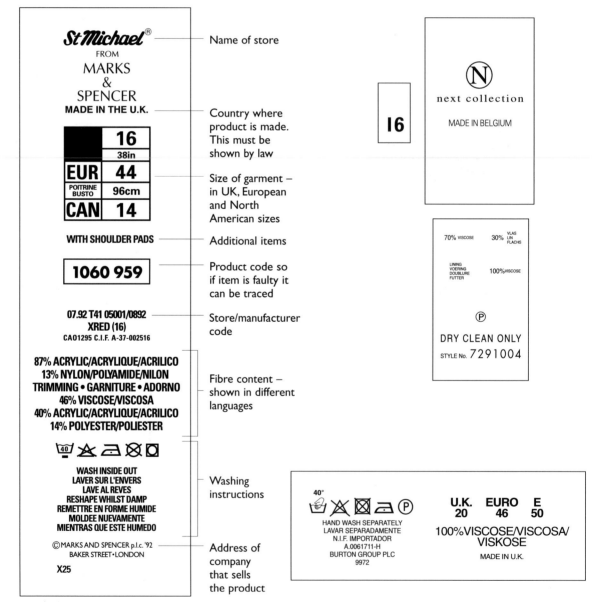

Information given on care labels

## Care labels on clothing

Care labels on clothing usually give the following information:

- company name or design logo
- country of origin
- fibre content
- garment size
- laundering instructions, eg dry clean, machine wash or handwash
- product code to identify when and where the product was made
- special instructions
- a spare button, if appropriate.

Some garments have other special labels if they are made from special fibres or they have had any special finishes added to them, or they may have been made in a special way.

Specialist labels on garments

## Laundering textiles products

The Home Laundering Consultative Council (HLCC) liaises with the manufacturers and retailers of textiles products to produce the instructions and the symbols that are found on clothing and other textiles products.

| Washtub – wash at maximum machine action | Handwash only | Chlorine bleach may be used | Cool iron |

 Do not wash Do not use chlorine bleach Warm iron

A bar or broken bar below the wash tub means wash at reduced machine action

 May be tumble dried May be dry cleaned Hot iron

Washtub symbol found on cotton/polyester shirt. It shows the maximum temperature for washing

Do not tumble dry / Do not dry clean / Do not iron

Laundering symbols

# Textiles systems and control

## What is a system?

A system is made up of four parts:

1 What goes into the system is called the **input**. This starts the system.
2 What happens inside the system is called the **process.** This changes whatever goes into the system.

3 What happens at the end of the process is the **output.** The end result or output must meet the specification.
4 **Feedback** checks if the output is correct. This is what controls the system. One way to check if the system has worked is to **test** the product, or to see if the product looks the way it is supposed to.

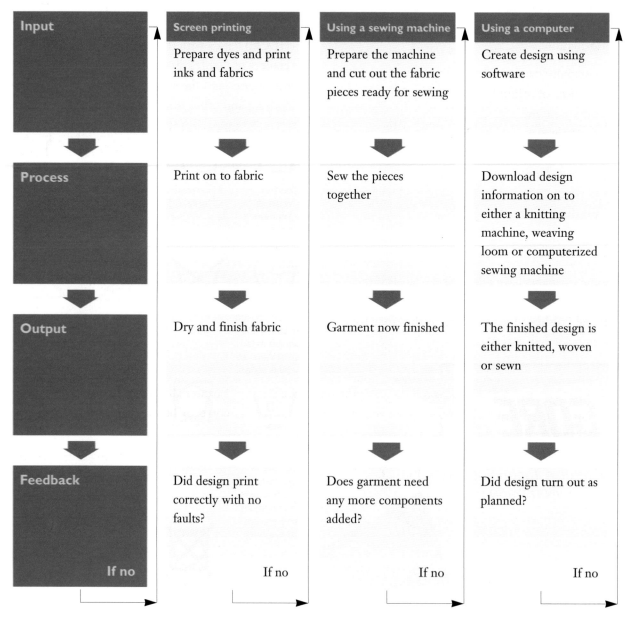

| Input | Screen printing | Using a sewing machine | Using a computer |
|---|---|---|---|
| | Prepare dyes and print inks and fabrics | Prepare the machine and cut out the fabric pieces ready for sewing | Create design using software |
| Process | Print on to fabric | Sew the pieces together | Download design information on to either a knitting machine, weaving loom or computerized sewing machine |
| Output | Dry and finish fabric | Garment now finished | The finished design is either knitted, woven or sewn |
| Feedback | Did design print correctly with no faults? | Does garment need any more components added? | Did design turn out as planned? |
| If no | If no | If no | If no |

The way a system works

# Why feedback?

Systems need to be controlled in order to make sure that the textiles product being produced is made to the correct standard and in safe conditions. Each of the controls can be checked at any stage in the making process. Controls include the following:

- **Process and production control** checks that the steps in the making process, such as laying out fabric, cutting out pattern pieces, sewing up garment panels, are correctly followed.
- **Quality control** is used to make sure the product meets set quality checks.
- **Health and safety controls** cover the correct and safe way to use equipment, and make sure that the environment is safe to work in.

- **Cost control** ensures that there are no hold-ups in production, as well as controlling the costs of different components.
- **Colour control** controls the standards of the colours used in the dyeing process.

## Questions

**1** Choose three different textiles products and make a system chart for each one.

**2** Describe three ways in which the textiles industry uses control systems. Why are control systems important?

| Control system | Textiles technology | Textiles industry |
|---|---|---|
| **Process and production** | To make sure you do not waste fabrics or materials | Ensures fabrics are correctly measured and tested and wastage kept to a minimum |
| **Quality** | Decide on critical checkpoints before you start work | Ensures that checks at critical points detect faults and are put right |
| **Health and safety** | Use equipment correctly and safely, and report all accidents | Staff trained in correct use of the equipment they are working on |
| **Cost** | Cost all the components needed to complete your project | Ensures all orders are costed correctly before production stage |
| **Colour** | Test your dyes using a multi-fibre strip | Sampling and testing ensure that colours are correct for each new dye batch |

How control systems are used in textiles technology and the textiles industry

# Planning a textiles product

It is important to prepare and plan your work in advance. You should do this when you start your design ideas. Fibre producers plan their work up to six months ahead of the textile designers. In turn they plan their design work up to 18 months ahead of fashion designers who plan their work around the fashion shows which are approximately six months apart. When textile products are to be made they are fitted into a planning schedule for the year or a particular season.

These are some of the things you will need to think about when planning your work:

- costs
- type of fabric/fibre content/yarn
- number of colours in the design
- equipment and materials needed
- length of time it will take to complete your work
- gathering all your equipment and materials together
- how easy you find it to use the equipment
- safety rules and regulations
- allowing time for research
- checkpoints at each stage of your work
- design development ideas
- knowing exactly what you are going to do.

This planning list will change order depending on what stage of the design, planning or making process you are at. Plans are important because they help you to make sure that you are making the product correctly, and in the same way each time.

## Checking your progress

You can check your progress by using a planning line.

A planning line

# Ways of presenting your plan

**Front view**

**Back view**

Stages in making up a jacket – using a numbered diagram

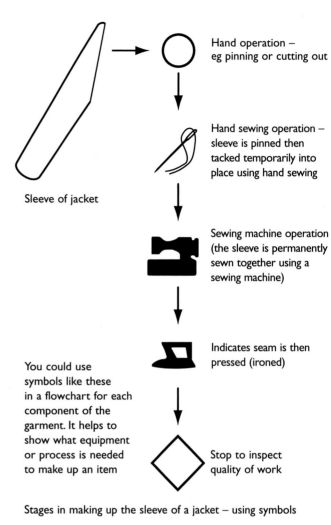

Sleeve of jacket

Hand operation – eg pinning or cutting out

Hand sewing operation – sleeve is pinned then tacked temporarily into place using hand sewing

Sewing machine operation (the sleeve is permanently sewn together using a sewing machine)

Indicates seam is then pressed (ironed)

You could use symbols like these in a flowchart for each component of the garment. It helps to show what equipment or process is needed to make up an item

Stop to inspect quality of work

Stages in making up the sleeve of a jacket – using symbols

## To do

**1** List the stages to make a patch pocket for a jacket. Show these stages using :

**a** a numbered diagram
**b** symbols.

For each stage list the quality and safety checks that you might carry out to ensure that the pocket is made correctly.

**2** Choose a textiles product and study it closely. You may have to disassemble it. Make a flowchart showing the stages of making the product, using a numbered diagram or symbols.

# Making a textiles product

When making your product these are the things you need to do:

- Use the right tools.
- Use the right equipment.
- Use the correct materials.
- Experiment with creating shapes.
- Try different methods of making up textiles products before starting on the final product.

You should check your progress as you make your product.

> **Checkpoint**
>
> I've finished planning. Now I need to look at making

> **What do I need to think about?**
>
> - joining fabrics together
> - adding colour to fabrics
> - choosing the right tools and equipment
> - using new machinery
> - trying new ideas
> - working safely and knowing the safety rules
>
> Try out some or all of these processes

> **Checkpoint**
>
> Evaluate the work you have done

Checking your progress

> **Also look at**
>
> - finishing techniques
> - IT and CAD/CAM
> - making large numbers of the product
>
> How does this affect my design?

> Prepare plan of work
> Decide on materials, equipment and processes

> **Checkpoint**
>
> Evaluate your product
> Does it match the design brief?
> Does it need improvements? If so, why?

## What is an evaluation?

Evaluation means to find out or to assess something in order to make a decision, which will help you to decide your next step. In the design process you will often be asked to do an evaluation, for example:

- in trying to see how a product is made
- by looking at designs of the past, the things that worked and the things that did not
- by assessing designs that you have done to see whether or not you need to make changes
- by checking test results to enable you to make decisions about the work that you have done
- by looking at your finished design to see whether or not you have completed it according to the original design brief and specification.

**A** Garden gloves

**B** Protective fire fighting clothing

## To do

**I** Look at photos A–H and answer the questions below:

**a** For each of the products create a product specification. To help, look back at the unit on writing a specification for a textiles product (pages 36–7).

**b** Why might you want to change anything about the designs shown? What would you add, take away or change? How would this affect the product, eg make it more wearable, safer, better value for money, etc?

**c** Choose one of the products and redesign it using the list you made above.

**C** A rucksack

**D** A tapestry

**F** Leisure clothing

**G** Baby's blanket

Creating product specifications for textiles products

**E** Knitted socks

**H** Jeans

# Modifying a textiles product

There are a number of reasons why you might want to adapt the materials or change the design that you are doing or change your method of work. For instance, you might decide to:

- choose a different fabric from the one you are using, eg use a knitted cotton jersey fabric instead of a plain weave cotton fabric
- change the components you are using, eg use Velcro instead of buckles
- alter the structure of the fabric before using it, eg add interfacing to strengthen your fabric, so that it will keep its shape for longer.

In the textiles industry a product may be modified before the production stage because it fails to meet the standard that is needed. Modifications are rarely made once a product has gone into full-scale production. Dyes may also be modified if the fabrics that are dyed come out 'patchy', where the dye does not reach all the fabric. The dye recipe will then be changed and a range of sample dyes will be tested until the fault is corrected.

## Why do textiles producers modify their textiles products?

The textiles industry is changing all the time. New fashions and styles come and go. To keep up with the current trends textiles producers modify styles from the previous season, or if the trend is for a new fashion they will use a particular era and recreate it, but give it a new look. The colour industry looks at colours from past seasons and modifies colours so they change only gradually.

The updated 70s look to the look of the 1990s

The look of the 1970s

How trainers have changed

## Modifying your own textiles products

1 Check that your design matches the design brief and specification that you created.

2 Fabric tests may show that a different fabric from the one you had originally chosen would better meet the needs of your design brief.

3 If the product you are making is a garment, you can first make it using a cheaper fabric. Try it on and if it does not fit, make alterations.

### Questions

**1** Look at the photographs. What differences do you see? Which do you think look like the original styles and which like styles that have been updated?

**2** Try to think of any other eras in textiles where textiles products were styled one way and then updated for another era. List some examples, and collect and analyse information about them.

### To do

Study some pictures and samples of different textiles products and explain how you would modify these products. How would your modifications affect the price of the product, or to whom the products were sold?

# Quality assurance and quality control

**Quality assurance** means building quality into a product from design to finish to try to ensure that only good quality goods are made. Quality assurance involves everyone working together as a team, to produce a quality product.

**Quality control** involves looking at specific areas where faults may arise and then setting up control systems to stop them happening. Many companies use the **BSI (British Standards Institution) standards** to control the processes that take place during production to ensure that all products are made to a certain standard all the time. Quality controls are usually applied to the production process of the garment and not to its design. Quality control inspectors check garments throughout the production stage to make sure that they are being made according to the specifications given.

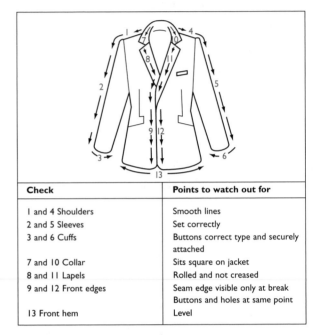

| Check | Points to watch out for |
|---|---|
| 1 and 4 Shoulders | Smooth lines |
| 2 and 5 Sleeves | Set correctly |
| 3 and 6 Cuffs | Buttons correct type and securely attached |
| 7 and 10 Collar | Sits square on jacket |
| 8 and 11 Lapels | Rolled and not creased |
| 9 and 12 Front edges | Seam edge visible only at break |
| | Buttons and holes at same point |
| 13 Front hem | Level |

A jacket is checked – using a quality control sheet
Source: *Introduction to Clothing and Production Management* by A J Chuter, Blackwell Scientific Publications, 1995

## What can go wrong?

| Woven fabric | Knitted fabric | Printed fabric | Garments/accessories |
|---|---|---|---|
| Ends (**weft** threads) broken | Uneven yarn | Print design misaligned | Stitching comes undone |
| Picks (**warp** threads) broken | Uneven dyeing | Smudging of print | Overlocking not done correctly |
| Uneven yarn | Holes | Colours do not match | Trim sewn on unevenly |
| Holes in fabric | Snagged yarns | Holes in fabric | Seams open or do not match |
| Uneven dyeing | Pattern with rows missing | | Patterns and stripes do not match |
| Too much shrinkage | | | Buttons fall off |

Some of the faults that can occur during production

The chart shows some of the most common faults that can occur. The important thing to remember is that if faults are left uncorrected, the retailer might be sent a faulty product which the manufacturer would then have to replace.

## Tolerance

To overcome the problem of faulty products manufacturers build tolerance levels into their fabric and garment specifications which set out the limits within which a product may be made. For example, if the seam allowance – the measurement of the seam from the stitch line to the edge of the fabric – is 1.5 cm with a tolerance of 0.5 cm, it means that the seam must fall within 1–2 cm from the seam edge to be accepted. If, however, the seam measured either 0.5 cm or 2.5 cm from the seam edge, it would be outside the tolerance level and would be rejected because it failed to meet the specification.

The chart below is an exemplar fabric specification noting down acceptable tolerances (If the fabric delivered failed to comply with the specification given, then the buyer would reject the fabric or ask that fault to be rectified).

| | |
|---|---|
| Fabric type | Polyester/wool worsted fabric |
| Length | 70 m + 10 m must give total length of 350 m |
| Actual length | must not be less than stated on the invoice |
| Width of fabric | 150 cm ± 1cm (150 cm + or - 1 cm) |
| Weight of fabric | 200 grams per m = 15 |
| Ends per cm | 25 per cm + 1 (25per cm + or - 1) |
| Picks per cm | 25 per cm + 1 (25per cm + or - 1) |
| Weave structure | 2/2 twill weave |
| Fibre content | 65% polyester, 35% wool |
| Shrinkage allowance | 1% in warp and weft (using standard test) |
| Shade | according to sample given |
| Surface properties | according to sample given |

Source: *Fashion Design and Product Management* by H Carr and J Pomeroy, Blackwell Scientific Publications, 1992

# Packaging textiles products

Some textiles products are packaged to protect them, especially when they are being transported from the factory to the retailer. The packaging will give a range of information, including:

- the maker's name
- a swing ticket with company logo or other details
- the size of the garment
- safety warning if a plastic bag
- any special features
- a price label or ticket which also includes details of the size and type of garment.

This type of packaging is usually made of a clear film to allow the customer to see the goods.

Swing tickets and price labels

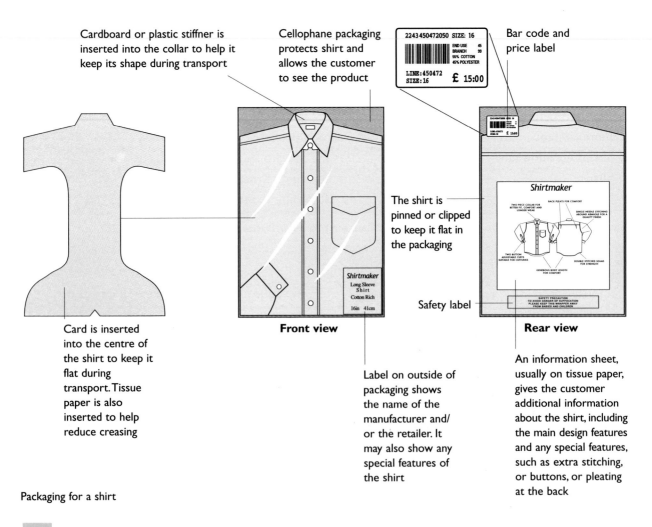

Cardboard or plastic stiffner is inserted into the collar to help it keep its shape during transport

Cellophane packaging protects shirt and allows the customer to see the product

Bar code and price label

The shirt is pinned or clipped to keep it flat in the packaging

Safety label

**Front view**

**Rear view**

Card is inserted into the centre of the shirt to keep it flat during transport. Tissue paper is also inserted to help reduce creasing

Label on outside of packaging shows the name of the manufacturer and/ or the retailer. It may also show any special features of the shirt

An information sheet, usually on tissue paper, gives the customer additional information about the shirt, including the main design features and any special features, such as extra stitching, or buttons, or pleating at the back

Packaging for a shirt

The retailer will also pack customers' purchases in carrier bags to enable customers to carry their goods home easily. The carrier bag acts as a form of advertising for the retailer. Carrier bags are often quite bright and eye-catching and usually have the logo or name of the retailer on the bag. They can be made out of a variety of different types of material such as plastic, card or paper.

**To avoid danger of suffocation do not give this bag to babies or young children**

Safety warnings

Carrier bags

## Price tickets

Price tickets on garments usually include a bar code. This allows manufacturers and retailers to log sales of a particular type of garment, or fabric, on to a computer. From this they can gauge how well a product is selling or which colours or styles are selling the best, and increase or reduce production or stock as a result.

## Packaging and safety

A lot of packaging comes with safety warnings and should not be given to young children.

### To do

**1** Collect a range of packaging from different types of clothing. What does each tell you about the product? What types of material is the packaging made from? Display some examples. Does the type of packaging used reflect the value of the product that was purchased?

**2** Collect a range of carrier bags from different types of shops or stores. Describe what each one looks like and the information it may contain. What do the carrier bags tell you about the shop, or the person who might purchase goods from that shop?

**3** Develop your own ideas for a range of packaging. Choose a shop or store, look at its packaging, evaluate it, then design your own. You could use a CAD, drawing or paint computer program to help you do this.

# Marketing textiles products

The textiles market is very competitive with everyone within the industry trying to sell their products. In order for products to be sold they have to be advertised in a way which will attract buyers.

## Points to consider when marketing products

- Who are you selling to?
- What will be the selling price of the product?
- Where will the product be used?
- What colours will be used?
- What is the added value in the product, eg type of finish, special trimming?
- Are you aiming
  an existing product at an existing market, or
  an existing product at a new market, or
  a new product at an existing market, or
  a new product at a new market?

When a new range of products is being designed, the designers have to look at the market that they are aiming at. They can do this by looking at consumer lifestyles or at people's social groupings which are based on the types of jobs that people do.

### To do

Using the list of points to consider, choose an existing textiles product. Decide which area of the market the product is aimed at. Now redesign the product, aiming it at a new market. Write a short report discussing your redesigned product.

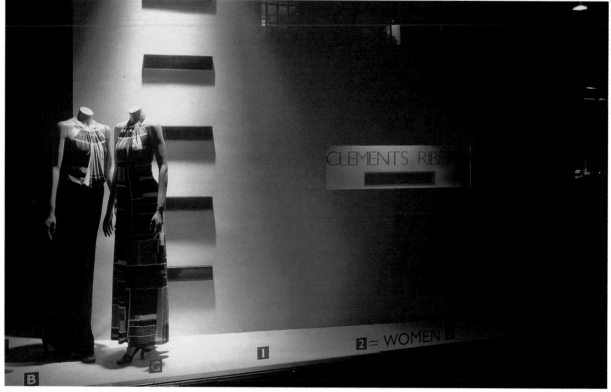

An eye-catching shop-window display

# The Burton Group

| Name of store | Age range |
| --- | --- |
| Burtons | 18–35 |
| Debenhams | 35+ |
| Dorothy Perkins | 18–35 |
| Evans | 25+ |
| Harvey Nichols | 35+ |
| Principles | 25–35 |
| Principles for Men | 25–35 |
| Top Man | 15–24 |
| Top Shop | 15–24 |

Fashion retailers in the Burton Group and the age range at which each one targets its products

A Burton shop

The Burton Group produces a range of goods for its various high street shops such as Top Man, Dorothy Perkins, and so on. The company used information on changes in the age groups of the population over the last few years and also looked at predicted age groups of the future to help it to target its markets accurately.

A Principles shop

'The Burton Group has a portfolio of retail brands targeted at most sectors of the population. Top Shop and Top Man are targeted at 15–24-year-olds, Principles and Principles for Men are targeted at the 25–35-year-olds, Harvey Nichols and Debenhams are aimed at the 35-year-olds. When the youth market was at its peak in the 1970s Burtons invested heavily in Top Shop and Top Man. As this "baby boom" generation grew older, Burtons placed emphasis on Principles and Principles for Men in the 1980s. More recently Debenhams has been the target of new investment in recognition of the progressive ageing population.'

Source: *The Business and Marketing Environment* by A Palmer and I Worthington, McGraw-Hill, 1992

## Questions

**1** Why did the Burton Group invest heavily in Top Man and Top Shop during the 1970s?

**2** Which chain of shops did it invest in in the 1980s, and which stores are receiving investment in the 1990s? Give reasons.

# Advertising textiles products

Manufacturers and retailers use advertising to promote their textiles products. The spider diagram shows the range of places where they may advertise. Some types of advertising may be more suitable for one type of product than another. Companies choose the best way for their products to reach the target audience.

## Selling textiles

A wide range of textiles products can be bought from a variety of different retail outlets. This gives consumers a choice about where to purchase their goods, which can be anything from furniture to clothing and the types of stores where goods can be purchased. The chart opposite shows where textiles products may be bought.

### To do

Collect one sample of each of the ways of advertising shown in the spider diagram. Choose one of the areas and design your own advertisement promoting the textiles product of your choice.

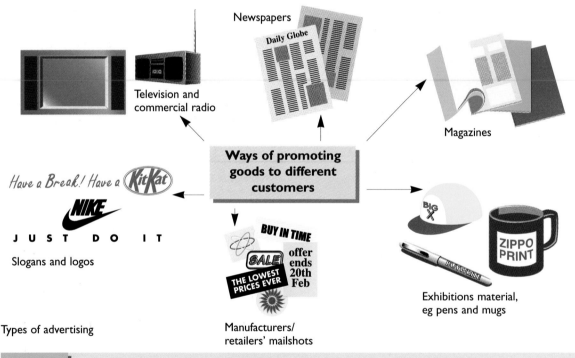

Television and commercial radio

Newspapers

Magazines

**Ways of promoting goods to different customers**

Slogans and logos

Types of advertising

Manufacturers/retailers' mailshots

Exhibitions material, eg pens and mugs

### To do

**1** Collect as many pictures as you can showing a range of textiles products. Group your pictures to match up with the different retail outlets shown in the chart. What things do you notice in the types of products that can be sold? Think about things like price of goods and quality. Write a report on your findings.

**2** Design a textiles product for a store of your choice. Create a range of posters to advertise your product.

**3** Collect different types of advertising information for textiles products. Choose one type of advertising and describe how it sells the product to the consumer.

| Retailer | Definition | Products sold | Customer |
| --- | --- | --- | --- |
| Independent | Fewer than ten shops. | Range of clothing of particular types | 30+ age group |
| Multiple | Usually a chain of shops owned by large company | Sell either specialist products (eg Mothercare, Olympus Sport) or range of products (eg Marks & Spencer, BHS) | 25+ age group |
| Department store, eg John Lewis, Allders | Usually a large shop on several floors | Range of products including clothing | 25+ age group – clothing can be expensive |
| Superstore | Large out-of-town site | Women, men's and children's wear and also other products | 25+ age group |
| Discount store | Shop, warehouse or industrial unit | Budget range of clothing | 18–25 age group. Customers on a budget |
| Co-operative store | Large store where employees are members | Limited range of clothing | 25+ (aimed at customers already shopping in the store) |
| Mail order company, eg Next, Littlewoods, Freemans | Customers purchase goods from an advert or catalogue by phone or post. The goods are delivered to the customer's homes | Wide range of products | 25–45 age group |
| Concession | Rents space in a department store | Particular makes of clothing | 25–40 age group, mainly customers looking for exclusive labels |
| Franchise, eg Benetton, Dash, Oasis | A large company gives an individual the right to sell its goods under its name | Various products | 18–35 age group depending on the product |
| Street market | Located in many towns. A small trader selling goods from a stall | Any type of clothing. Not always high quality, can also be second-hand/recycled | All age groups |

Where textiles products can be bought

# Textiles for specific needs

Textiles have many uses and can be adapted to meet the needs of specific situations. In developing textile products you will need to explore other cultures and how they use textiles, as well as finding out about how textiles are used in industry.

As you will have seen, textiles can be used for almost anything, and in many different ways. The ways in which textiles can be used may be broken down even further. For example, indoor clothing can be broken down into many more categories.

## To do

Look at the spider diagram showing where textiles are used. For each area name three textiles products that have been designed specifically for this use.

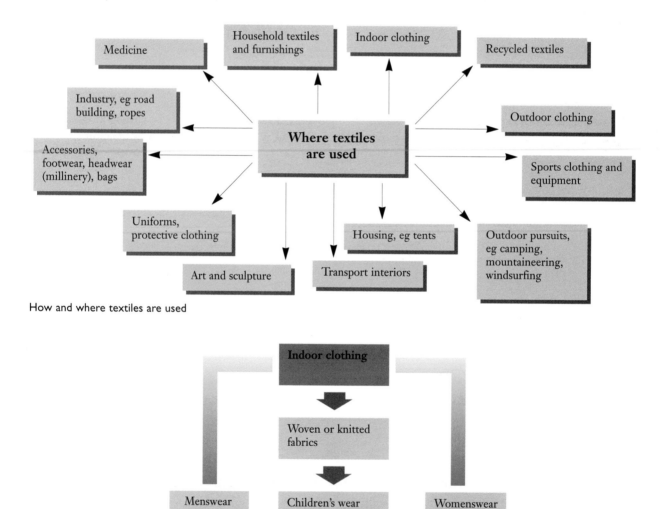

How and where textiles are used

Indoor clothing

**1** For each of the areas shown in the indoor clothing diagram name two or three examples of textiles products. Draw one of these textiles products. You can use pictures from magazines and catalogues or look up information on the product you have chosen on a visual database on CD-ROM. Label all the features.

**2** Using the information you have gathered, choose one product and try to find out as much information as you can about it. For example, is the fabric knitted or woven, printed, dyed, bonded or laminated? Has it had any special finishes added? Does it use special construction techniques? Does it need to have special tests before it can be used?

You could also consider the many uses of textiles in relation to the country where you live, culture, religion, climate, the type of occasion or the physical characteristics of the country. Each product made from textiles has a function depending on who it is for, how it will be used and where it will be used.

**To do**

Explore how textiles products are used in other cultures. You may want to look at how products are manufactured, as well as what influences the design of the products that they use. Use the headings below to guide you.

| Country | Main textiles product | Main methods of putting pattern on to cloth | Main methods of adding colour | Symbols and motifs used in design |
|---|---|---|---|---|
| India | The sari (women's clothing) | Weaving and embroidery | Dyeing and batik | Nature and religious symbols |
| Peru | | | | |
| Ghana | | | | |
| China | | | | |

**To do**

Sometimes people who have physical disabilities need textiles products, that have to be specially adapted to their way of living.

**1** Can you think of any special things that need to be taken into consideration when making these types of products?

**2** Design a range of 'prototype' textiles products that can be used by people with physical disabilities. Compile a report of your findings. Collect as much information as you can.

# Textiles and the environment (1)

During the 1980s designers such as Katherine Hamnett started to promote the use of unbleached, natural-coloured cottons and fabrics as a way of encouraging care of the environment through the use of natural textiles.

A Katherine Hamnett design – 1997

A garment in Tencel

Each year the textiles industry uses thousands of tonnes of water in the processing and finishing of its products, and it is known that many of the dyes and chemicals used pollute the environment. But this is beginning to change. New finishing techniques are being introduced whereby water is reused throughout the dyeing and finishing processes, and new dyes are being produced that are less toxic. A new fibre, Tencel, designed with the environment in mind, is being manufactured by the textiles company Courtaulds. Garment manufacturers are also recycling plastic bottles to produce PET which is made into fleece jackets.

## Recycling textiles products: patchwork

The recycling of textiles products is not something new. Textiles have always been recycled. The craft of patchwork became popular during the late 1400s when, during a bitterly cold winter, instead of throwing away fabric, it was cut up into shapes and made into large covers. The art of patchwork spread and the designs became more intricate. Patchwork covers became prized family possessions and were passed from one generation to the next. The art continued as people migrated to the New World (America) during the seventeenth and eighteenth centuries, and designs became more elaborate, using geometric shapes that were linked together to form patterns. The designs created were used as a way of telling the history of a family or to commemorate special events. The main fibre used to create patchwork was cotton because of its hardwearing properties. Although almost any type of fabric can be used, the decision on which one to use is based on the end use of the product being made. Today, items using patchwork are used not only for clothing or bedding but also as wall-hangings or sculpture.

Patchwork can be used with appliqué and hand or machine embroidery or printing and dye techniques. One way is to create a length of patchwork made out of white fabric with different fibres, then dye it. The fibres will all take to the dye differently. This can then be printed on to, or decorated in different ways.

## To do

**1** Using a range of geometrical shapes, create a range of designs based on the craft of patchwork. You can make templates (shapes that you can draw around) using card, or use a computer paint or drawing program to create designs. Use different colours and textures to create patterns of different sizes. Decide how you can then use your designs on textile products.

**2** Look at the techniques of developing patchwork design ideas by combining different techniques and skills that you have learnt.

Patchwork quilt designs

# Textiles and the environment (2)

## The fashion of recycling

Today, patchwork is not only a craft pastime; it is also used in the recycling of clothing, where fabrics are cut up and used to make complete garments. The use of patchwork as a clothing design feature can be seen in the clothing of the 'hippie' era of the late 1960s and early 1970s and was seen again in the 'grunge' look of the late 1980s and early 1990s, both of which were influenced by the music of the times.

'Hippie look'

The grunge look of the 1980s

Over the past ten years, the recycling of clothing has become big fashion news. Today, all sorts of clothing and accessories can be recycled and reused to create new garments that are affordable and allow you to be creative. An example of a company that does this is the Midlands-based Scrap Scrap, a clothing recycling firm which remodels clothes by taking them apart and reusing the fabrics that are still of good quality. It supplies several high street shops with its recycled products.

Here are some other ways in which you can recycle textiles:

- Cut up old clothes for patchwork or appliqué work.
- Remodel clothes by taking them apart and reusing the fabric.
- Donate unwanted clothing to a charity shop, where it will be sold to raise money for a charitable cause.
- Reuse buttons, trimmings, zips and fastenings.
- Wool jumpers that have not been treated with a finish to stop them shrinking can be felted by washing them in hot water. Once they are dry, cut them up and use them to create other types of clothing or accessories.
- Take unwanted clothing to a clothes bank for recycling. Many are situated next to supermarkets and can usually be found near the paper and can recycling areas.
- Fabrics can be cut into strips and used to create 'rag rugs' or 'hooked-rugs'.

Lizzey Reakes is a textile designer who uses recycled fabrics to create 'rag rugs'. Her rag rugs can be used as conventional floor rugs, or they can be displayed as wall hangings. An example of her work is shown below.

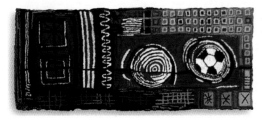

Recycling clothing – rag rugs. Design by Lizzey Reakes.

## What can I learn from recycling clothes?

Some clothes or other textiles products do not have care labels on them. This makes it difficult to identify them. You would be able to tell whether they were woven, knitted or non-woven, but you might not be able to say what the fibre content was.

In order to recycle fabrics, you will need to disassemble them and this will allow you to see the number of pieces needed to make the item, as well as the trimmings and other components that make up the item.

# Using information technology

Information technology (IT) can be used in many ways in your textiles technology work. The spider diagram shows you some of them.

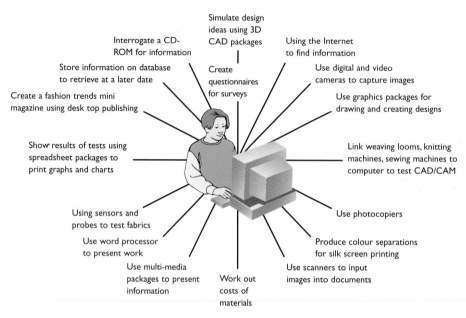

- Simulate design ideas using 3D CAD packages
- Interrogate a CD-ROM for information
- Using the Internet to find information
- Store information on database to retrieve at a later date
- Create questionnaires for surveys
- Use digital and video cameras to capture images
- Create a fashion trends mini magazine using desk top publishing
- Use graphics packages for drawing and creating designs
- Show results of tests using spreadsheet packages to print graphs and charts
- Link weaving looms, knitting machines, sewing machines to computer to test CAD/CAM
- Using sensors and probes to test fabrics
- Use word processor to present work
- Use photocopiers
- Use multi-media packages to present information
- Produce colour separations for silk screen printing
- Work out costs of materials
- Use scanners to input images into documents

How computers are used in textiles technology

## Why use IT in textiles technology?

The computer is another tool that you can use in textiles technology. The following are some computer programs which can help you to plan, design and make your work:

**1** Specialist textiles software, eg Designaknit 6 for Windows, allows you to create knit design ideas. It gives simulated knit images, calculations for yarn amounts and instructions for knitting. You can design your own garment styles or you can use patterns already on the system. It will also allow you to import patterns from other software packages.

**2** Fittingly Sew for Windows allows you to create your own designs for patterns for clothing. You can also do simulated pattern layouts and calculate fabric requirements. All your information can be printed for later use.

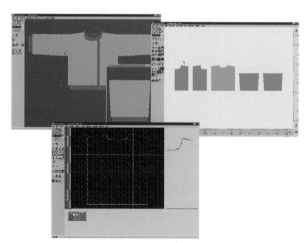

Designaknit 6 for Windows

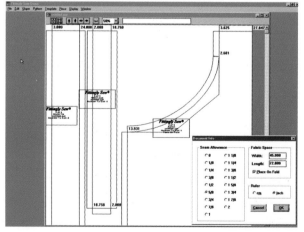

Fittingly Sew

**3** Corel DRAW packages from V3 (V7 now available) allow you to do lots of textures and patterns and get good effects. Adobe Photoshop is also a good graphics package, especially when working on scanned images.

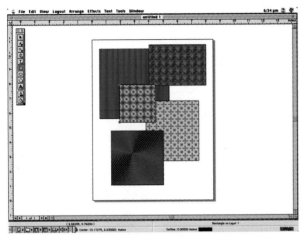

Designs using Corel DRAW

**4** Speak Easy allows you to speak directly into a word processing package using a microphone and it will automatically print your speech on the computer monitor. You can then save your work.

**5** 3-D simulation packages, eg AutoCad and AutoSketch, allow you to draw pictures of rooms with all types of furniture. You can then use your own designs to 'decorate' the rooms.

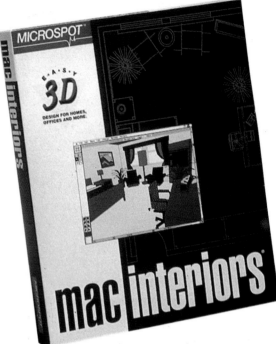

3-D simulation computer software package

## To do

**1** Working in groups of three or four, use a desk top publishing package or word-processing package to create a mini fashion magazine that focuses on the following:

**a** Present the results of a survey of the types of clothes teenagers like to buy; the amount teenagers spend on clothes every month; the largest amount of money teenagers have spent on a single item and what the item was; their opinions on the next trend in fashion. Illustrate your article using a spreadsheet.

**b** Write a short article on the work and designs of a famous designer of any type of textiles product. Illustrate your article.

**c** Include a survey of the types of shops in your area and the kinds of clothes they sell.

**2** Using a database package combined with a scanner, create a database which focuses on textiles fibres and their uses. Illustrate your database information with pictures of fibres and how they are used.

**3** Create a range of fabric designs. The fabrics can either be woven, printed or knitted, and you can choose the season you want to design for. The finished design should also include two or three colourways.

# Using IT and CAD/CAM in the textiles industry

In industry computers are used in the design and manufacture processes in the following ways:

- designing fabrics and patterns
- databases for storing information
- planning work through a factory
- creating colour separations for screen printing
- creating elaborate embroidery stitches and patterns
- operating machinery
- spreadsheets for costing information
- information for delivery of stock
- the automatic transfer of manufacturing information between the office and the factory – this is called computer integrated manufacture (CIM)
- sewing machines with built-in patterning programmes, that can also be connected to computers to enable designs to be adapted
- the transfer of EPOS (electronic point of sale) information from retailer to head office to manufacturer, allowing companies to respond quickly to changes in the market
- the use of modems and the Internet to transfer information from one part of a company to another and also all over the world.

**Computer-Aided Design (CAD)** – allows the designer to create a design on a computer just as an artist would draw using a pen or a pencil. The computer gives the designer access to tools that can help provide information quickly.

**Computer-Aided Manufacture (CAM)** – the computer is used to help in the manufacturing process. For example, the computer works out the most economical way to lay patterns for the bulk cutting of fabric and the information is then downloaded to an automatic fabric cutter.

The system

Pattern planner at work

Completed lay plan

Computers in the garment industry, by Lectra Systems

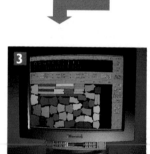

Adapting a design on a computer screen with a special pen

**Computer Integrated Manufacture (CIM)** – allows manufacturing information to be transferred between the office and the factory floor so that planning details and production can be monitored closely.

## Questions

**1** What do the letters CAD, CAM and CIM stand for, and what do these terms mean?

**2** Name five ways in which computers can be used in the textiles industry.

**3** How does the use of computers help the textiles industry?

**Shima Seiki Europe, with offices in Milton Keynes, Leicester, Carluke and Bangor, Northern Ireland**

The Japanese knitting company Shima Seiki is at the forefront of technology in its use of CAD/CAM.

Computers are used throughout the design process, from producing yarn and garment design ideas to visualising the finished garment. Computer images can be used to present garments without the need to show actual knitted fabrics, enabling buyers to decide before knitting which fabrics they want as well as the garment style.

The company's latest technical advance in Japan is the 'Knit Factory Boutique' where customers can walk in and design their own jumper and have it customised to fit them. It costs between 15,000 and 30,000 yen (approximately £75–£150) and the finished jumper can be collected within the week.

Computer aided design – 3-D simulation of knitted jumper by Shima Seiki

# Design and make a fashion garment

Fashion is all about wearing the clothes that make you feel good. The clothes you wear can say something about you and your likes and dislikes. Fashion can be created by almost anyone and can be influenced by things like music, art, styles and clothes of the past. When designers are looking at creating new ranges in clothing styles they will often look at fashions of the past to give them some ideas. They will also look at techniques of the past and adapt them for today's use. One such designer is Vivienne Westwood, who bases much of her fashion and fabric designs on designs of the past.

## A history of the waistcoat

The waistcoat is one of those garments that has been in fashion for over 300 years. In recent years waistcoats have become a fashion item and what had become an essential part of a man's suit is now worn by both sexes.

A waistcoat design by Vivienne Westwood

1680s

1770s

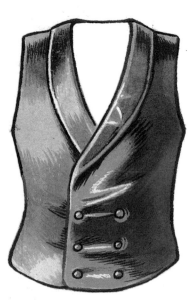

1850s

The changing styles of waistcoats

1940s

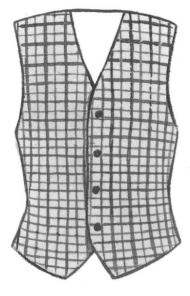
1960s/1970s

1990s

The changing styles of waistcoats (continued)

## Questions

Study the pictures to see how the style of the waistcoat has changed.

**a** What do you notice about colours and pattern styles?

**b** What types of fabrics do you think would have been used for these garments?

**c** How do you think you can use this visual information?

Waistcoats were first seen in men's dress around the late 1660s during the reign of King Charles II and were described as 'a dress after the Persian mode and the Eastern fashion of vest'. The 'vest', as the waistcoat became known, is the term that is still used by traditional (bespoke) tailors of today. It was worn originally by men of the nobility and upper classes, but was slowly adapted for men of all social classes. The waistcoat first became fashionable for women around 1770 when it was adapted as part of outerwear, and was worn as part of day and riding wear.

By the 1800s the waistcoat was an essential part of men's clothing and was highly decorated with embroidery. It was usually made of silk or velvet and was worn both during the day and evening. By the early 1900s the male waistcoat had become more formal, and was made of fabrics that matched suits for daywear. More elaborate waistcoats were worn only as part of eveningwear.

By the 1940s waistcoats were again being worn by women and were part of the 'utilitarian' wear of the war years. Because of the war, restrictions had been put on the amount of material that could be used to make clothes. New styles emerged after the war and the waistcoat was then only worn by men to work.

The late 1960s and early 1970s once again saw the waistcoat become an essential fashion item. Today waistcoats are worn by a wide variety of people for different reasons, eg as a fashion accessory by any age group, or as a uniform for paramedics or soldiers. The waistcoat has also been adapted and made into various types of protective garments, eg the life jacket. It has even been adapted for use on animals.

*Continued on next page*

## To do

### Design brief

A major high street store is creating a whole range of casual and more formal wear for 11–14-year-olds to complement the range of designs that it already has. In particular, it wants to create a range of waistcoats that reflects the interests of teenagers and that can be used for a variety of different occasions. The price of the finished garment should be £15.99.

You may decide to do this project on your own, or you can work as a small group, forming your own design team and working out a production chain system for making more than one garment.

## Getting started

These are some of the things that you will need to know as you design and make your product:

- which equipment to use
- sewing skills, whether by hand or using a sewing-machine
- how to join fabrics together
- how to make buttonholes
- how to attach fastenings
- how to make a garment template, first in paper and then in the form of a toile
- how to adapt a garment template to fit
- produce a plan of work
- dyeing and printing techniques
- embroidery and other forms of decoration such as patchwork and appliqué.

## Check your progress

Use the chart as a guide to help you to check your progress. You may want to add more categories as you decide how to plan your work.

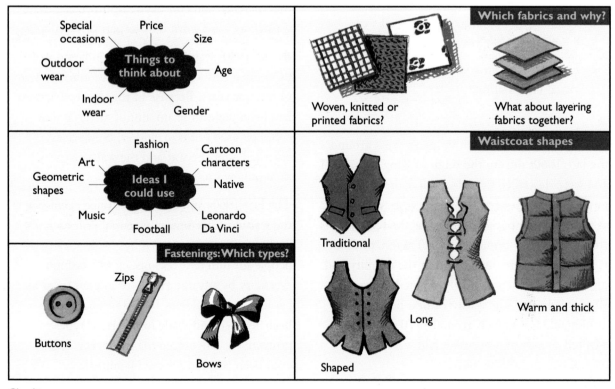

Checking your progress

**1. Design brief**

- Analyse the design brief – pick out key words
- You may decide to invite an outside speaker to talk to you, eg a designer

**2. Research**

- What type of research do I need to do?
- Where will I get my information?
- Do I need to plan a special trip anywhere?
- What type of marketing information do I need?

**3. Evaluation of information**

- Evaluate the information gathered
- Decide what to do next
- Think about health and safety rules

**4. Mood board**

Create a mood board to include:

- fabric samples
- trimming and buttons
- pictures showing where you got your ideas from

**8. Surface decoration techniques**

- Appliqué
- Patchwork
- Embroidery

**7. Surface pattern techniques**

Test printing/dyeing techniques

**6. Tests**

Test seams, pockets, joints, fastenings

**5. Fabrics**

- Look at choice of fabrics
- Test fabrics
- Create fabric/fibre profile

**9. Evaluation**

- What are my decisions?
- What do I need to do?

**10. Design ideas**

- Based on information, choose final idea
- Start working out costs

**11. Final design**

- Design pattern
- Create sample garment (toile)
- Modify garment as necessary

**12. Quality control**

- Check quality
- Check against specification
- Check tolerance levels

**16. Make your garment**

**15. Evaluation**

Make sure that all the equipment you need is available and that you know how to use it safely

**14. Plan of work**

Create plan of work. Include information about what equipment you need at each stage of the making process as well as information about quality checks

**13. Components**

Decide on final fabrics and trimmings

**17. Check progress**

- Keep a diary of your progress
- Record your progress using cameras or drawings

**18. Evaluate progress**

If working in a team, decide if there are things you need to check

**19. Complete your work**

**20. Final evaluation**

Present your work. What about a fashion show?

Progress chart

# Design and make fabrics for interiors

## The history of fabrics for interiors

One of the earliest uses of fabrics in the home was to keep in the warmth. Fabrics were also used as screens for privacy. The nobility and upper classes decorated their walls with fabric instead of wallpaper to show how wealthy they were. The Industrial Revolution of the eighteenth and nineteenth centuries, saw a rise in mass production; this meant many more people were able to buy an increasing variety of fabrics, and wallpapers became more and more fashionable.

William Morris was one of the best textiles design artists of the nineteenth century. He said, *'On the whole one must suppose that beauty is a marketable quality and that the better the work is all round, both as a work of art and in its technique, the more likely it is to find favour with the public.'* Many of Morris's designs were printed by hand and many of the techniques he created for printing are still used today.

One of the textile designs by William Morris

Fabric can be used for a wide range of interior purposes, from furnishings and wall-hangings to seat covering in cars and on public transport.

Wall-hanging designed by Philip O'Reilly

## Designing fabrics for interiors

Many designers produce their finished designs on paper and also present a drawing of the interior showing how their fabrics might be used. The latest computer software allows designers to design fabrics on screen, where they can see the fabric displayed in different colourways. A texture mapping or 'drape' feature shows how the fabric might look when draped over upholstery, and special printouts allow the designer to see what the fabric might look like.

## Techniques for fabrics for interiors

All the following techniques can be used when producing fabrics for interiors:

- appliqué
- patchwork
- embroidery by hand or machine
- printing
- weaving
- knitting
- recycling fabrics.

Design ideas for a printed fabric by textiles designer Linda Nottingham

*Continued on next page*

| Fabric type | How is colour added | End uses |
|---|---|---|
| Woven fabric | Fibre and yarn can be dyed<br><br>Fabric can be dyed in 'greige' state<br><br>Fabric can be printed using various methods<br><br>The warp yarns of woven fabric can be dyed in a process called 'ikat'<br><br>Weaving<br><br>Surface pattern can be added using embroidery and decoration | Curtains, bedding<br>Upholstery for interiors<br>Car/transport interiors<br>'Fiberart' for art galleries<br>Textiles hangings |
| Knitted fabric | Fibre and yarn can be dyed<br><br>Fabric can be dyed in 'greige' state<br><br>Can be printed on using a variety of methods but best suited to finer knitted fabrics<br><br>Surface pattern can be added using decoration | Upholstery<br>Car interiors<br>Textile hangings |
| Printed fabric | Colour can be added using a dyeing or printing process | Curtains, bedding, lampshades, etc<br>Car/transport interiors |
| Felted fabric/bonded fabric | Colour can be added to the fibre before it is felted and then the felted fabric can be decorated/embroidered and also printed | Decorative art and wall-hangings |

How fabrics can be used for interior design and the ways in which colour may be added

## To do

**Design brief**

Design a fabric for use in an interior. The finished item can be used as a decorative object or have a specific use, and can be used in either the home or work environment. You may use one single technique or combine two techniques together. You should show two or three colourways of your finished design.

You will need to include information on fabric tests you have carried out; as well as master research information.

You may decide to do this project on your own, or you can work as a small group.

# Getting started

The chart shows some of the skills and knowledge that you will need as you design and make your product:

## Designing skills

Research relevant information

Analyse the design brief

Prepare specifications for:

- fabric requirements, colours, method of printing
- fabric type
- trimmings or fastenings
- type of sewing thread to be used
- type of dyes and print pastes

Produce plan of work with testing points/quality control for each stage of the design process

Explore different techniques and examine ways in which you can design fabrics for interiors

## Making skills

Join fabrics together

Use correct tools and equipment

Try out techniques that you may need to use to make your item

Assess whether or not it is possible to make your product in large quantities

Add a finishing process to your product

Find out views of others about the product that you have designed

## Evaluation

Consider testing methods you used and why

Analyse the information you gathered

Think about different ways of presenting your finished design work, eg comparing paper designs with designs done using computers

Analyse your costing information using a computer spreadsheet program

Give reasons for the type of fabric to be used

Analyse results of using printing pastes and dyes on different fabrics (see page 23)

Consider whether you would have to change your design if you had to make your product in large quantities

## Things you should know

Choose a theme and decide where you could get information for an idea

Understand how colours are selected and grouped together so you can choose colours for your design

Be aware that the number of colours used will affect the cost of the design – the more colours used, the higher the cost

Understand that **repeat patterns** (see page 32) are the final version of your design painted to the exact specifications of the print process. The layout of the final print will ensure that when the pattern is printed it will flow in a continuous pattern and you should not be able to see where the design joins

Understand how IT can be used in designing your product

## Check your progress

Use the chart on page 83 as a guide to help you check your progress.

# Design and make an accessory

## What is an accessory?

An accessory is an extra item used to complete an outfit. Some accessories are essential, such as shoes, others are simply for decoration, such as jewellery and scarves. Some fulfil a need and are decorative at the same time, eg umbrellas and gloves.

## Types of accessory

Shoes, bags, scarves, gloves, jewellery, ties, handkerchiefs, socks, hats and handbags come in different shapes and sizes. They are made from a wide range of fabrics which may have special finishes depending on the end use of the accessory and can be decorated in many ways, eg with logos and emblems.

## A history of the handbag

The handbag is a universal accessory, usually carried by women, but over the years it has been adapted to suit the times.

Handbags for women first appeared around 1790. The fashion of the time was for flimsy dresses ('robe en chemise') which were made from lightweight muslin cambric or calico, a finely woven cotton fabric. The dresses were so lightweight that pockets were impractical, as they would weigh down the garments, making them go out of shape, so small bags were designed for women to carry around the small articles they needed. These small bags or 'reticules' were rectangular in shape and were opened and closed with a drawstring.

Today bags come in all shapes and sizes and are not only carried by women but also used by men. They are used for many purposes, eg cool bags for keeping food cool in hot weather and changing bags for carrying baby equipment.

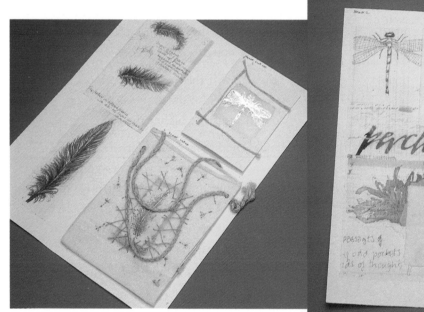

Design ideas for bags by textiles designer Linda Nottingham

One well-known manufacturer of bags and suitcases is the French company of Louis Vuitton. Its products are made by hand and are very expensive.

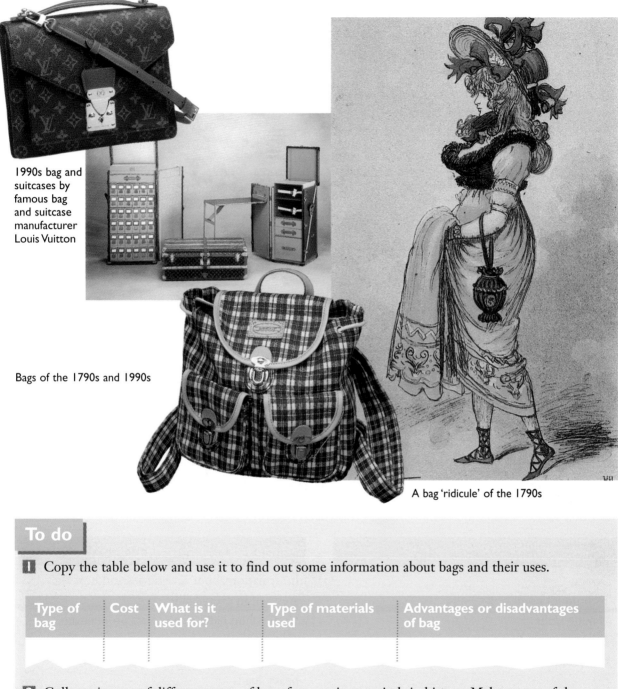

1990s bag and suitcases by famous bag and suitcase manufacturer Louis Vuitton

Bags of the 1790s and 1990s

A bag 'ridicule' of the 1790s

## To do

**1** Copy the table below and use it to find out some information about bags and their uses.

| Type of bag | Cost | What is it used for? | Type of materials used | Advantages or disadvantages of bag |
|---|---|---|---|---|
|  |  |  |  |  |

**2** Collect pictures of different types of bags from various periods in history. Make a note of the different ways in which the bags open/close, the types of materials used for fastenings and the styles of the bags.

**3** Find out about the history of other types of accessories. How have they changed over the years?

*Continued on next page*

## To do

### Design brief

A new sportswear company wants a range of accessories to complement the sportswear and outdoor adventurewear that it has created for the 18–25 age group. It is particularly interested in the following accessories:

- hats – these must keep the head warm, but allow the skin to breathe
- bags – these must be functional, with lots of pockets, and be able to carry up to 3 kg without breaking
- socks – these must have lively patterns and be made from a durable fibre combination
- scarves – these should be able to change from scarves that go around the neck to become head coverings or have an alternative use, eg become a mat to sit on.

You have been asked to design and make one type of accessory.

You may decide to do this project on your own, or you can work as a small group.

## Getting started

The chart shows some of the skills and knowledge that you will need as you design and make your accessory.

### Designing skills

Create specification
Follow design brief
Work out costings
Create prototypes
Decorating different fabrics

### Making skills

Join fabrics together
Strengthen fabrics
The use of seams and fastenings

### Evaluation

Design
Techniques used
Making skills
Tests conducted
Fabrics used

### Things you should know

Information about accessories and how they are used in everyday life
Understand batch/mass/craft production
Testing fabrics for strength and durability
Testing threads used that can withstand heavy loads
Advertising your product
Conducting market research

## Check your progress

Use the chart on page 83 as a guide to help you check your progress.

# Textiles and the law

As with all other products that are bought, textiles products need to be of 'merchantable' (saleable) quality and be fit for the purpose for which they are to be used. There is a range of services available to help you should you have a problem with your goods, but the law is also there to protect the consumer. Certain textiles products have to carry special warnings:

- Furnishing fabrics must display fire warnings to show that these items have passed tests or that you need to be aware.
- Some items of clothing must display special signs, eg children's nightdresses must be treated to make them less flammable and all nightwear must display the warning 'Keep away from fire'.

Fire warning on a furnishing fabric

The chart on page 92 shows some of the laws that protect consumers when they purchase goods. Apart from legislation to protect the consumer, there are also agencies that provide protection and promote standards that goods should be aimed at.

*Department of Prices and Consumer Protection* – a government department set up to offer help and advice

*Consumers Association* – produces the consumer magazine *Which?* which carries out tests on goods and compares similar types of goods

*The media* – specialist consumer TV and radio programmes and magazines offer help and advice on varied consumer issues

*Office of Fair Trading (OFT)* – a government body set up to oversee anything to do with consumer law and protection

*Citizens' Advice Bureaux* – offer free advice and help in all sorts of matters

*Design Council* – looks at British goods only and 'approves' those showing a high standard of design

*Trading standards officer* – employed by the local authority. Can supply information about consumer laws and consumer protection. Also investigates reports by members of the public about faulty goods or services or anything else related to the consumer

*British Standards Institution (BSI)* – produces a series of standards that ensure that products are fit for the purpose for which they are intended

*Professional and trade associations* – consist of people who work in a particular industry, and who can give advice about the products that their members make

*Continued on next page*

| Act | What protection does it give |
| --- | --- |
| Resale Prices Act 1964 | Suppliers cannot impose minimum prices, but can suggest a manufacturer's recommended price (MRP)<br><br>Suppliers cannot refuse to sell to a retailer |
| Trade Descriptions Act 1968 | It is an offence to falsely describe goods or services offered for sale. This applies to written and spoken descriptions |
| Fair Trading Act 1973 | Set up the Office of Fair Trading to provide protection for consumers and business people |
| Consumer Credit Act 1974 | Aimed at protecting consumers from credit companies<br><br>Protects the consumer from misleading credit advertisements |
| Consumer Safety Act 1978 | Regulates the sale of goods that might be dangerous, such as electrical goods |
| Sale of Goods Act 1979 | Goods must be of merchantable quality<br><br>Goods must be as described<br><br>Goods must be fit for the purpose for which they are to be used |
| Weights and Measures Act 1985 | Quantity of contents must be marked on packaging by number<br><br>It is an offence to give short weight or inadequate quantity, or to mark goods with the wrong amount |
| Consumer Protection Act 1987 | It is an offence to give misleading prices for goods<br><br>The Act also applies to special offers |
| Sale and Supply of Goods Act 1994 | Reinforces the 1979 Act stating that goods must be fit for the purpose for which they are sold |

Consumer protection laws

## Questions

**1** Why do we need laws to protect the consumer when they purchase goods from a store?

**2** Name 3 professional associations that protect the consumer, when they purchase goods from a shop.

**3** Using the Sales of Goods Act 1979 as a guide, design a poster that shows how the consumer is protected by law, when purchasing goods.

# Clothing and textiles design and the law

At least two or three times a year, major fashion and textiles companies produce collections of their latest designs which they show at fashion shows in cities around the world such as London, New York, Paris and Milan.

The designers take great pride in their work, but very often they find that their designs have been copied or adapted and are on sale before they have had a chance to sell them to stores around the world. Many designers do not allow their work to be copied and this includes not only the garments but also the company logo that might be used to promote their goods.

It is not only clothing that is copied but also fabric designs and trimmings that are used on garments. If designs are copied without permission then copyright is said to be infringed.

## How do designers protect their designs?

- By dating and signing their work or original drawings. It is important to note that only the drawing is copyright, not the finished garment, although if the copy is exactly the same as the original or has only been slightly changed, then copyright infringement has taken place.
- When a design is made it can be registered with a bank or solicitor and dated to say that it is an authentic design.
- Many designers register their work with the Patent Office but this can only be done if the design contains innovative ideas or processes.

Logo designs and designer garments

# Glossary

**analyse** to break down a given task into smaller parts

**bespoke tailoring** a traditional and labour-intensive method of making clothes, especially suits (custom-made clothing)

**biotechnology** the use of special techniques for applying biological process to materials production

**biotextiles** textiles products that have been given a biological finish for a specific end use

**blended fibres** two or more fibres mixed together into a single yarn

**bonded fabrics** a method of making fabric by layering, fusing or matting fibres together using heat or adhesives or chemicals (see *non-woven fabrics*)

**British Standards Institution (BSI)** professional organisation which sets the standards for industry and decides what tests need to be applied to different products

**care labels** labels on textiles products that give information about the fibre content, laundering instructions plus any other relevant information

**characteristics** the main features of a textiles fibre, yarn or fabric

**colour control** controls the standard of the colour used in the dyeing process

**colourfast** a dyed product that does not 'run' when washed

**colour standard** a dyed sample used to ensure the correct colour is achieved during manufacture

**Computer-Aided Design (CAD)** designs created using a computer

**Computer-Aided Manufacture (CAM)** a computer used in the manufacturing process

**Computer Integrated Manufacture (CIM)** the automatic transfer of information between a company's head office and its factory

**conversion** the process of changing fibres into yarns and then into fabric

**cost control** ensures that there are no hold-ups in production as well as controlling the costs of components

**cost price** the price paid by the retailer for goods

**cut, make and trim (CMT)** the process of cutting out and making up and finishing of a textiles product

**deconstruction** taking apart of a textiles product (see *disassembly*)

**design attributes** the visual and tactile properties of a textiles product

**design brief** short statement about the task to be solved

**design proposal** see *design brief*

**design specification** the specific design details which a product has to match

**disassembly** taking apart or breaking down a product to see how it is made

**dyeing** the process of applying colour to a textiles product which is soaked in a coloured solution

**ends** see *warp threads*

**fabric specification** the specific details needed to make a fabric

**feedback** checks if the output in a system is correct

**fibres** fine hair-like structures which can be natural, synthetic or regenerated and can be long (filament) or short (staple)

**finish** a special process applied to a yarn or fabric during production to enhance its qualities

**flying shuttle** a spinning machine invented in 1733 by James Hargreaves

**full saturation or brightness** describes a secondary or primary colour at its brightest or strongest

**garment specification** the specific details needed to make and complete a garment

**geotextiles** textiles products that are used in the ground

**gin** the process of breaking up the cotton fibres after harvesting

**greige (grey) goods** textiles products before colour is added

**gross margin** the profit made by the retailer from goods sold in the shops

**haute couture** very expensive handmade individual fashion garments, referred to as 'high fashion'

**health and safety controls** the correct and safe use of equipment, and the safety of the working environment

**hues** another name for colour

**input** the information that goes into a system to start it

**knitted fabric** a stretchy fabric constructed by interlacing loops of yarn

**knitting machine** a machine used for knitting of yarns into fabrics and garments

**loom** a machine used to produce cloth by weaving

**manufacturing specification** the specific manufacturing details and instructions needed to make a product

**manufacturing stage** the process of making up a product; the number of operations needed to make a product

**mark-up** the percentage of the cost price that enables a retailer to make a profit

**mass-produced goods** goods that are manufactured on a large scale

**microfibres** very thin hair-like fibres or filaments

**mixed fibres** the mixing of different types of yarns in a fabric

**modify** to make slight changes to a product

**mood or image board** used to display initial ideas for a design

**mordant** a chemical used in dyeing to help attract dyes to fibres

**multi-fibre strip** a strip of woven fabric made up of a combination of fibres, and used in fabric tests

**non-woven fabrics** a fabric made up of layers of fibres which are strengthened by being bonded together using heat or adhesive or mechanical or chemical means

**output** the end result of a system which must meet the specification

**parameters** to work within given limits

**picks** see *weft threads*

**primary colours** red, yellow and blue

**printing** the process of adding colour to the surface of a fabric using a screen, stencil or block

**process** what happens inside the system

**process and production control** checks the steps in the making process

**product specification** the specific production details which a product has to match

**production parameters** set details or limits to work within

**production stage** the stage at which all the details are worked out before a product is put into production

**profit margin** the difference between the selling price and the cost price

**properties of fibres** the main features of a fibre

**quality assurance** the method of assuring quality of a product from design through to manufacture

**quality control** looks at where faults may arise and sets up controls systems to stop them happening

**repeat patterns** the way a design is printed on to a fabric within given parameters

**research** finding out information

**resist method** method of applying a wax or starch paste to a fabric before dyeing. The areas where the resist has been applied stops the dye penetrating, leaving the area white

**retail price** the price that goods are sold at in the shops

**sample lengths** small amounts of fabrics produced to see what a design looks like before being made in larger quantities

**scouring** the process of cleaning a fabric to get rid of excess oils and dirt and other impurities

**secondary colours** combination of the primary colours to form another colour, eg red and yellow = orange

**selling price** the price charged in the shops for goods

**sewing machine** a manual or automated machine used for sewing

**shade** produced when black is added to any colour

**spinning** a process of making fibres into yarns

**spinning jenny** a spinning machine invented in 1764 by Richard Arkwright

**spinning mule** a spinning machine invented in 1769 by Samuel Crompton

**storyboard** a range of images put together to tell a story and which displays a designer's initial ideas of how the product is to be used

**'S' twist** the direction of twist put into a yarn during spinning

**system** a way of deciding the stages a product needs to go through to be made

**tactile properties** how a product feels

**tertiary colours** a combination of primary and secondary colours

**test** a process to ensure that standards are met

**textiles designer** a person who designs fabrics

**theme board** a display of ideas related to a certain theme

**tint** produced when white is added to any colour

**toile** a sample garment made from cotton calico

**tolerance level** to work within given limits

**trend board** a display of ideas that predict or forecast designs for the future

**value** the lightness or darkness of a colour

**visual properties** how a textiles product looks

**warp** the vertical threads in a woven fabric

**water frame** a spinning machine invented in 1769 which used water as its power source

**weaving** a method of producing fabric by interlacing warp and weft threads

**weft** the horizontal threads in a woven fabric

**wholesale goods** goods that are made on a large scale

**wholesale price** the price paid for goods by the retailer

**William Morris (1834–96)** a famous textiles designer and artist

**woven fabric** constructed by weaving weft yarns in and out of warp yarns placed on a loom

**yarns** a length of fibres and/or filaments with or without twist

**'Z' twist** the direction of twist added to a yarn during spinning

# Index